SOLOMON
TO THE EXILE

Studies in Kings
and Chronicles

SOLOMON TO THE EXILE

Studies in Kings
and Chronicles

by

John C. Whitcomb, Jr.

BAKER BOOK HOUSE
Grand Rapids, Michigan

Copublished by
Baker Book House and BMH Books
© 1971 by BMH Books

First printing, January 1971
Second printing, August 1972

ISBN: 0-8010-9516-6

Library of Congress Catalog Card Number: 72-152379

PHOTOLITHOPRINTED BY CUSHING - MALLOY, INC.
ANN ARBOR, MICHIGAN, UNITED STATES OF AMERICA
1972

To
NORMA
my beloved wife
and to our children
DAN, DAVE, TIM, DON, CONNIE, and BOB

ACKNOWLEDGMENTS

The author wishes to express special appreciation to the following individuals who made valuable contributions to the preparation and production of this volume:

Mr. Robert Ibach, Jr., Library Assistant for Grace Theological Seminary, who prepared the chronological charts, the maps, the photograph captions, and the bibliography; and who carefully read the entire manuscript for the purpose of checking style and Biblical references.

Dr. John J. Davis, Associate Professor of Old Testament and Hebrew, Grace Theological Seminary, who read the entire manuscript and made helpful suggestions.

Dr. Benjamin A. Hamilton, Assistant Librarian, Grace Theological Seminary, who prepared the Name Index and the Scripture Index.

CONTENTS

LIST OF ILLUSTRATIONS

Photo Credits

Matson Photo Service, Alhambra, California 91803

The Oriental Institute, University of Chicago, 1155 East 58th Street, Chicago, Illinois 60637

The New Bible Dictionary, © Inter-Varsity Fellowship, London, England, published in U.S.A. by Wm. B. Eerdmans Publishing Company, Grand Rapids, Michigan 49502

TRANSLITERATION

Whenever possible, Hebrew and Greek words have been transliterated according to the following form:

Greek	Consonants	Vocalization
α — a	א — '	___ — ā
∝ — a	ב — b, b̲	___ — a
ε — e	ג — g, g̲	___ — e
η — ē	ד — d, d̲	___ — ē
o — o	ה — h	___ — ê
ω — ō	ו — w	___ — i
ζ — z	ז — z	___ — î
	ח — ḥ	
θ — th	ט — ṭ	___ — o
ξ — x	י — y	___ — û
ν — u	כ — k, k̲	___ — u
φ — ph	ל — l	___ — ( )e
χ — ch	מ — m	
ϒ — ps	נ — n	___ }
' — h	ס — s	___ } ( )ᵃ
	ע — '	
	פ — p, p̲	
	צ — ṣ	
	ק — q	
	ר — r	
	שׂ — ś	
	שׁ — š	
	ת — t, t̲	

PREFACE

The following chapters make no claim to being a detailed study of the Books of Kings and Chronicles. The claims and counter-claims of higher and lower critics are conspicuous for their absence. Instead, it has been the author's purpose to come to grips with the essential teaching of each consecutive passage from the middle of I Kings to the end of II Kings, comparing it to Chronicles and then the rest of Scripture (and occasionally the insights of archaeological discovery) to determine exactly what happened in this fascinating period of Israel's history and what these events mean to us today.

The informal style is a reflection of the living context out of which these studies flow. It has been the author's great privilege to "search the scriptures daily" with graduate students at Grace Theological Seminary for the past twenty years. Solomon stated that as "iron sharpeneth iron; so a man sharpeneth the countenance of his friend" (Prov. 27:17). If such interaction in the study of Old Testament history has been God's means of equipping some of these men to expound His Word more effectively to His people, it has also been His means of challenging this writer to dig ever deeper into the sacred text to discover precious and vital aspects of His revelation.

The history of the Divided Kingdom of Israel from Solomon's glorious reign to the destruction of the northern tribes by the Assyrians and the southern tribes by the Babylonians is almost incomparably fascinating and rewarding to the reverent student. Here we find a bewildering array of kings and prophets and clashing nations; and yet through it all may be seen the guiding hand of One who changes not and who accomplishes unerringly His sovereign and redemptive purposes in history.

The author has approached the Old Testament text with the full confidence that the original words (which have been marvellously and providentially preserved through the centuries) were inspired of God and therefore absolutely inerrant. This concept was taught by our Lord Jesus Christ (Matt. 5:18; John 10:35) and His apostles (II Tim. 3:15-17; II Peter 1:19-21), and is everywhere assumed in the Old Testament. It is hoped that the student will bring to this study an open Bible and a heart that is ready to submit to its truth (Acts 17:11). It is only in this way that the Spirit of God can bring forth "things new and old" from the inexhaustible resources of His written revelation.

John J. Davis
Winona Lake, Indiana

"Open thou mine eyes, that I may behold wondrous things out of thy law" (Ps. 119:18).

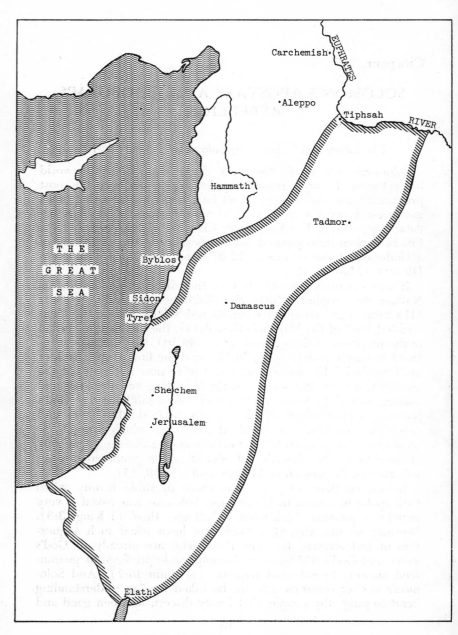

1. The Empire of David and Solomon

Chapter 1

SOLOMON'S APOSTASY AND JEROBOAM'S REBELLION

The Glory and Wisdom of Solomon (I Kings 3—10)

Solomon's was surely the most glorious kingdom the world has yet seen. It was certainly not the largest, nor even the most prosperous, but the wisdom of its king and the perfection of its government and the quality of its religion made it glorious beyond comparison. The Lord Jesus Christ paid indirect tribute to this fact when he compared Solomon's glory to the perfection of a God-created flower (Luke 12:27) and Solomon's wisdom to His own (Matt. 12:42).

It seems entirely possible, in fact, that discerning men such as Nathan the prophet, Ahijah the Shilonite, and Iddo the Seer (II Chron. 9:29) could have considered Solomon to be the long-awaited Seed of the Woman (Gen. 3:15), the Shiloh from Judah in the prophecy of dying Jacob (Gen. 49:10), the Star and Sceptre of Balaam's vision (Num. 24:17), and the final House Builder of II Samuel 7:13. Judah and Israel were now as "many as the sand which is by the sea in multitude, eating and drinking and making merry" (I Kings 4:20), an apparent fulfillment of God's promise to Jacob (Gen. 32:12 — "I will surely do thee good, and make thy seed as the sand of the sea, which cannot be numbered for multitude"). Furthermore, Solomon practically claimed to be the Messiah in Psalm 72, as he pondered the significance of the Queen of Sheba's visit (72:10, 15).

In one of those very rare occasions in Bible history when God spoke to a man in his dreams, Solomon was asked a very searching question: "Ask what I shall give thee" (I Kings 3:5). We may be sure that God would not have asked such a question of just anyone, for only those who are already in God's grace and God's will have the incomparable privilege of guaranteed answers to universal requests (cf. John 15:7). And Solomon's answer confirms this, for he asked for "an understanding heart to judge thy people, that I may discern between good and evil" (I Kings 3:9; cf. James 1:5). God not only granted that specific request, but added riches and honor as well (I Kings 3:13), providing the perfect historical example for Jesus' promise that if we seek the kingdom of God and His righteousness first, "all these things shall be added unto you" (Matt. 6:33). Solomon's wisdom apparently did not include any details of God's prophetic plan for Israel and the nations, but it was unparalleled in the realms of jurisprudence (I Kings 3:28), administration (I Kings 4:20, 29; 5:12), poetry (I Kings 4:32), natural science (I Kings 4:33), architecture and engineering (I Kings 5:1—7:51; 9:15-22), and commercial enterprise (I Kings 9:26—10:29).[1]

In the midst of all this glory and wisdom, however, one fatal weakness remained — a sinful human nature. Solomon had wisdom, wealth, and power. But he was a sinner! At the end of his life he sadly confessed: "Surely there is not a righteous man upon earth, that doeth good, and sinneth not" (Eccles. 7:20). This is exactly why he could never have crushed the serpent's head (Gen. 3:15) and thus fulfill mankind's basic need of a Redeemer (Job 19:25). As Solomon's glory faded, and his royal successors brought great disillusionment to the godly remnant, prophets began to point more and more to the coming of an Ideal King who would neither sin nor fail (cf. Isa. 9:6, 7). Not Solomon, but the Christ, would fulfill God's ultimate purpose for His people.

Multiplying Wives (I Kings 11:1-8)

During the first twenty-four years of Solomon's reign it might appear that Pharaoh's daughter was his only wife (cf. I Kings 3:1; 6:37—7:1). This might be concluded from the statement in 11:1 that "Solomon loved many foreign women, together with the daughter of Pharaoh." And this would be a highly desirable interpretation, for God does not approve of polygamy (Matt. 19:5) and He blessed Solomon marvellously during those years. On the other hand, it must be recognized that God had also

---

[1]For an analysis of these aspects of Solomon's reign, see the previous study in this series: John J. Davis, *The Birth of a Kingdom* (Grand Rapids: Baker Book House, 1970), pp. 169-190.

richly blessed David during the early years of his reign, and that in spite of a polygamous household (II Sam. 3:1-5; 5:12-16). Furthermore, the Song of Solomon implies a God-honoring relationship between Solomon and the Shulamite maiden at a time when he already had sixty queens and eighty concubines (Song of Sol. 6:9, 13). Finally, Solomon must have married Naamah the Ammonitess a couple of years *before* he became king, and thus before he married Pharaoh's daughter, for Rehoboam was forty-one when Solomon died at the end of a forty-year reign (I Kings 14:21; II Chron. 12:13).[2]

Why did God permit David and Solomon to multiply wives? God had said to David through Nathan the prophet: "I gave thee thy master's house, and thy master's wives into thy bosom" (II Sam. 12:8). But this must be understood as God's *permissive* will, even as our Lord explained with regard to divorce: "Moses for the hardness of your heart *suffered* you to put away your wives: *but from the beginning it hath not been so*" (Matt. 19: 8). Not only did Moses specifically warn kings against multiplying wives to themselves (Deut. 17:17), but he also gave the tragic examples of multiple wives in the homes of Abraham (Gen. 16:1-6) and Jacob (Gen. 34:30; 35:21). Jealous wives (Gen. 30:16) and spoiled children (I Kings 1:6) were the inevitable fruit of polygamy, and Solomon had to lament over his son Rehoboam: "who knoweth whether he will be a wise man or a fool? yet will he have rule over all my labor wherein I have labored, and wherein I have showed myself wise under the sun" (Eccles. 2:19). Thus, God, in His providence, saw to it that both David and Solomon suffered severely for establishing polygamous households.

But the one consideration that must have overridden all others in the thinking of Solomon was the desire to establish diplomatic ties with the hundreds of city-states and kingdoms of the eastern Mediterranean and the Fertile Crescent. The most effective way to confirm a commercial or political treaty with a

---

[2]In the light of Abijah's statement that "Rehoboam was young and tender-hearted" (II Chron. 13:7) when he became king, some have suggested that instead of being forty-one, he was only twenty-one (compare II Chron. 36.9 with II Kings 24:8 for the age of Jehoiachin).

foreign king was to marry one of his daughters and give her a prominent position in the court. Theoretically a king would think twice before offending a father-in-law. This was a common and accepted practice among ancient rulers, and Solomon (contrary to the known will of God) conformed to this standard.[3]

However, multiplying wives was only the beginning of contradictions and disasters. Each wife, as a true representative of her father's kingdom, brought with her the religious paraphernalia and the priests of her god. As we shall see in Chapter 3, Jezebel brought with her from Phoenicia 850 prophets of Baal and Asherah when she came to Israel to be Ahab's queen (by arrangement of their fathers Omri and Ethbaal who planned thus to cement a political treaty).

Let us attempt to picture the situation that began to develop around Jerusalem during the last fifteen or twenty years of Solomon's reign. It must have been like Massachusetts Avenue in Washington, D.C., lined with the embassies and legations of many nations — little islands of foreign culture within the borders of the United States. A few years ago I visited this section of our capital city and walked into a fabulously beautiful Moslem mosque crowned with a white limestone minaret piercing the sky above. The costly structure was built with contributions from fifteen predominantly Moslem countries of Africa and Asia, so that there, on that 30,000 square-foot portion of American soil, the god Allah is officially honored!

So it was during Solomon's declining years. Shrines to pagan gods with attending priests and guardian queens dotted the hills surrounding Jerusalem. And there they remained for *three hundred years* — inviolable and untouched even during the reigns of such reforming kings as Asa, Jehoshaphat, Uzziah, and Hezekiah. At last, during Josiah's great reform movement toward the end of the seventh century B.C., these "high places" around

---

[3]The decipherment of the Nuzi tablets reveals that it was an accepted practice of Abram's day for a barren wife to give her handmaid to her husband to beget children that would be legally hers (Gen. 16:1; cf. K. A. Kitchen, *Ancient Orient and Old Testament*, [Chicago: Inter-Varsity Press, 1966], p. 154).

the city were destroyed (II Kings 23:13). And two centuries after that, Nehemiah pronounced God's sad epitaph on Solomon's folly: "Did not Solomon king of Israel sin by these things? yet among many nations was there no king like him, and he was beloved of his God and God made him king over all Israel: nevertheless even him did foreign women cause to sin" (Neh. 13:26).

The Rebellion of Jeroboam (I Kings 11:9-25)

In view of the enormity of Solomon's sin, it is remarkable that God showed grace toward him in two distinct ways. First, he was allowed to live out his days as the ruler of a united kingdom. Second, his son would be permitted to rule over part of the kingdom instead of losing it all (I Kings 11:12-13). This promise of grace both in time and extent of the judgment was really God's way of honoring the Davidic Covenant of II Samuel 7.

It is also fascinating to observe how God was preparing for the fateful day of kingdom division long in advance of Solomon's spiritual defection, and even before his reign began! For example, Hadad the Edomite fled to Egypt (I Kings 11:15-19) and Rezon of Syria rose to power even before David died (I Kings 11:23-25). God is never taken by surprise when men fail, but His resources of grace are more than sufficient for those who trust Him (cf. Rom. 5:20).

It can be demonstrated that Jeroboam's rebellion (I Kings 11: 26, 40) was the climax to a very extensive background of events in Israel's history. Jeroboam's tribe — Ephraim — was a very proud tribe. Joshua, the conqueror of Canaan, was an Ephraimite. The tabernacle was first located at Shiloh within their tribal boundaries; and, for that matter, one of the very first places where Abram built an altar in the Promised Land was within their territory, too (Bethel — Gen. 12:6-8). It was apparently for such reasons as these that the Ephraimites chided with Joshua about the small size of their territorial allotment: "Why hast thou given me but one lot and one part for an inheritance, seeing I am a great people, forasmuch as hitherto Jehovah hath blessed me?" (Josh. 17:14).

Later, when Gideon (of the tribe of Manasseh) defeated the Midianites by a spectacular and supernatural victory, the jealous Ephraimites chided him with these bitter words: "Why hast thou served us thus that thou calledst us not when thou wentest to fight with Midian?" (Judges 8:1). It was only by a soft answer that Gideon avoided a civil war then and there. But the Ephraimites did not fare so well when they denounced Jephthah of Gilead for not calling them to lead the battle against Ammon (Judges 12:1). A rugged frontiersman of illegitimate origin (Judges 11:1-3), Jephthah challenged their insufferable pride and cut off their retreat across Jordan by demanding the Shibboleth password, slaughtering 42,000 of them in the bloodiest civil strife in centuries. Thus subdued, the Ephraimites submitted to Philistine conquest and also to the reign of Saul of Benjamin and David of Judah.

But in the process of time the pride of Ephraim raised its head again. The colossal burdens of taxation and forced labor that Solomon imposed on all the tribes for building programs that centered largely in Jerusalem (I Kings 9:15), proved too much for Ephraim and other northern tribes. Although they were over-awed by the wisdom and glory of Solomon, smoldering resentment was nevertheless present according to their later complaint to King Rehoboam: "Thy father made our yoke grievous" (I Kings 12:4).

Jeroboam's Plot

It was against a background such as this that a young Ephraimite named Jeroboam came to the forefront. Ambitious and highly competent, he was soon placed by Solomon over the Ephraimite work crews that labored in Jerusalem. In consultation with his fellow workers an assassination plot was hatched, and Jeroboam went back to Ephraim to rally support. Ahijah the Shilonite met him on the way and confronted him with God's proposal. If he would desist from this murderous plot and honor the Davidic kings and Zadokian priests in Jerusalem, God would give him ten tribes and a perpetual dynasty in the north. This was a magnificent and gracious offer, but Jeroboam, like Ahaz two centuries later (cf. Isa. 7:11-12), was not content

with God's plan and provision. And this brought about his ultimate ruin. As it turned out, his plot was a failure (compare
I Kings 11:26b with 11:40a); and barely escaping with his life,
he fled to Egypt to bide his time.

The Division of the Kingdom

After the defeat of Absalom, David had unwisely contributed
to the inferiority complex of the northern tribes by favoring Judah at his triumphal recrossing of the Jordan (II Sam. 19:9-15).
Their pride thus wounded, the men of Israel denounced the
men of Judah (II Sam. 19:40-43), and then joined in the rebellion of Sheba. The battlecry of Sheba is interesting — "We have
no portion in David, neither have we inheritance in the son of
Jesse: every man to his tents, O Israel" (II Sam. 20:1). The expression as used here was idiomatic for "return to your homes."
Israel no longer lived in tents, but the memory of nomadic days
had not yet faded away. A half century later, the northern
tribes used the very same battlecry when Jeroboam led the
revolt against the dynasty of David and the kingdom was split
(I Kings 12:16).

Jeroboam was a very clever and industrious man. Utilizing
the building skills he had developed under Solomon (I Kings
11:28), he established two northern capitals: *Shechem*, near the
border of Ephraim and Manasseh at the location of Mount Ebal
and Mount Gerizim where Joshua had first dedicated the Promised Land to Jehovah (Josh. 8:30-35), and *Penuel* across the Jordan (I Kings 12:25). This trans-Jordan capital may have been
necessitated by the anticipated invasion of Pharaoh Shishak
(his former protector — I Kings 11:40), which occurred in the
fifth year following the division of the kingdom (I Kings 14:
25). Later on, for an unknown reason, he established another
west-Jordan capital at Tirzah (I Kings 14:17; 15:33).

Jeroboam's New Religion

The greatest challenge that confronted Jeroboam, however,
was not Egypt but Jerusalem. Three times a year, in accordance
with God's revealed plan, the nation went up to Jerusalem to
worship Jehovah (Lev. 23; cf. Exod. 23:17). As the Levites

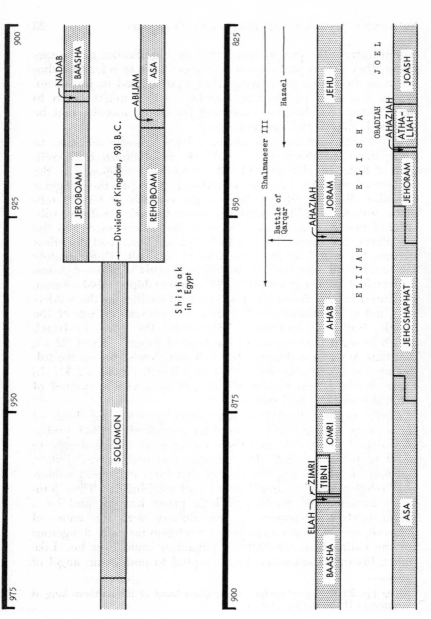

2. Time Chart: 975 to 825 B.C.

would instruct the people concerning the significance of the sacrifices, they would probably also take occasion to refer to Rehoboam as the legitimate Davidic king who reigned in Jerusalem.
Before long, the people from northern tribes might begin to
draw certain conclusions concerning Jeroboam, namely, that he
was both illegal and unnecessary.[4]

Filled with such fears, Jeroboam adopted drastic measures to
bring these influences to an end. He revolutionized the religion of Israel by changing (1) the symbols of religion, (2) the
centers of worship, (3) the priesthood, and (4) the religious
calendar. First of all, he changed the symbols of Israel's religion. Instead of golden cherubim above the ark, Jeroboam sub-
stituted two golden calves. Calves or bulls were sacred to the
Egyptians, and during his stay in Egypt Jeroboam had doubtless
become fascinated by the popularity of this cult. Unfortunately
for Israel, Jeroboam was able to find in the first high priest Aaron
a precedent for using a golden calf as a worship symbol. Aaron,
pressured by the demands of idolatrous Israelites in the wilderness, not only fashioned a calf from the golden earrings of the
people, but even exclaimed: "These are thy gods, O Israel,
which brought thee up out of the land of Egypt" (Exod. 32:4).
Not that Aaron was denying Jehovah completely; for on the following day he proclaimed a feast to Jehovah (Exod. 32:5). In
other words, Aaron presented the calf as a visible symbol of
Jehovah's strength and power.

In like manner, Jeroboam, determined to satisfy the desire of
the average Israelite for a spectacular symbol of his God, probably assured the people that these calves were intended only to
point to Jehovah. And, after all, this was nothing really new,
but was merely an amplification of that form of Israel's wilderness religion which Aaron himself had established! Thus Jeroboam assumed the position of high priest himself, and by a
clever mixture of popular pagan idolatry with the name of
Jehovah, brought forth a compromise religion far more dangerous
for the nation than out and out paganism could ever be. Like
Satan, his supreme master, he attempted to pose as an angel of

---

[4]See pp. 29-30, for an analysis of Abijam's taunt of the northern king as
recorded in II Chronicles 13:4-11.

light and a minister of righteousness (II Cor. 11:14-15), and thus succeeded in "slaying" his tens of thousands. Twenty-one times after this, Old Testament writers refer to Jeroboam as the one who "made Israel to sin" (I Kings 14:16, etc.).

In the second place, Jeroboam established two new worship centers at Bethel and Dan. These were clever choices, for *Bethel* ("house of God") had been Jacob's worship center where Jehovah had spoken to him twice (Gen. 28; 35). *Dan* was also significant because Jonathan, a grandson of Moses, had established there on the very northern extremity of the land a worship center and a dynasty of priests for the tribe of Dan during the many years that the tabernacle was at Shiloh (Judges 18:30-31). Why bother to go all the way to Jerusalem to worship Jehovah when these God-honored places, newly equipped with Aaron-style calves, were ready at hand?

Thirdly, a new religion demanded a new priesthood. It would be utterly futile to attempt to persuade Levites to function in such a context, so Jeroboam opened priestly privileges to the highest bidders. Even in the days of the Judges, when "every man did that which was right in his own eyes" (Judges 21:25), it was considered a special blessing to have a Levite for a priest (Judges 17:13). But now that the iniquity of the Israelites was becoming full, even this downward shift became possible (I Kings 13:13-14). Utterly disgusted at this drastic departure from divinely revealed tradition, the vast majority of priests and Levites fled southward to Judah, taking with them the remnant of true believers from the northern tribes and leaving behind them a situation of near-total apostasy (II Chron. 11:13-17).

In the fourth place, Jeroboam changed the religious calendar. To have no religious calendar at all would have been as foolish as to have no symbols, worship centers, or priests. A substitute religion, rather than no religion, has always been Satan's supreme goal (cf. Rev. 13). The seventh month, with its Feast of Trumpets (first day), Day of Atonement (fifteenth day), and Feast of Tabernacles (fifteenth to twenty-second days), was the climax of the religious year. So Jeroboam simply shifted the calendar one month ahead to the eighth month, "the month which he had devised of his own heart" (I Kings 12:33), doubtless making its ceremonies even more spectacular (if possible!) than its counterpart in Judah. In our own day, religious movements which possess the least Biblical truth often have the most elaborate ceremonies and the most impressive worship centers.

The Prophet from Judah (I Kings 13)

No matter how deep the spiritual darkness of Israel became, God always had a human channel available through whom His Word could be proclaimed. King Jeroboam was proudly burning incense on his new altar in Bethel, when an unnamed prophet from Judah burst upon the scene, announced that a future Davidic king named Josiah[5] would desecrate the altar (cf. II Kings 23:15-20 for the fulfillment 300 years later), and confirmed the spectacular prophecy with an equally spectacular sign. Jeroboam's effort to stop him was met with divine judgment, and his plea for mercy was met with divine grace; but in neither case did the king truly repent of his sins.

God had commissioned the unnamed prophet to utter his curse and return immediately to Judah without eating or drinking in the spiritually contaminated land of Israel (compare the somewhat similar experience of Amos at Bethel during the reign of Jeroboam II 200 years later — Amos 7:10-13). So when Jeroboam, deeply impressed with the prophet's supernatural powers and thinking that he could bribe him into using his magic to the advantage of the kingdom, offered him food and a reward, the prophet utterly refused. But the next test was too hard for him. An old prophet in Bethel, who probably had once served the Lord but had compromised away his spiritual usefulness, invented a message from God to deceive the prophet. Said he, "I also am a prophet as thou art; and an angel spake unto me by the word of Jehovah, saying, Bring him back with thee into thy house, that he may eat bread and drink water" (I Kings 13:18).

The prophet believed the trumped up message, accepted the invitation, and died under God's judgment as a result. Why was the penalty so severe? Was it really his fault? Our approach

---

[5]Another remarkable example of this type of prophecy was the naming of Cyrus 150 years in advance (Isa. 44:28; 45:1).

to this problem is exceedingly important. God's Word, from Genesis to Revelation, indicates clearly that it *is* possible to recognize God's voice through the convicting and illuminating work of the Holy Spirit. No other supporting evidence is really needed, or that would outweigh God's own voice in importance to the human heart. The unnamed prophet knew God's command. He also knew that God does not contradict His own Word. Therefore, as the Apostle Paul stated, "though we, or an angel from heaven, should preach unto you any other gospel than that which we preached unto you let him be anathema" (Gal. 1:8). So when a prophet said that an angel said that he *could* eat and drink in Israel, his heart should have detected the hiss of the Serpent and his lips should have cried out, NO! !

The fact that the old prophet was deeply touched by the unnamed prophet's testimony and punishment in no way modifies the tragedy of the episode. What Satan could not do by outward persecution, he accomplished through inward enticement. Not only the old prophet of Bethel, but all subsequent "sons of the prophets" in Bethel, Gilgal, Jericho, and elsewhere must have pondered this vivid lesson whenever they ministered the message of the Holy One of Israel.[6]

The End of Jeroboam's Dynasty

We are surprised to learn that Jeroboam had a godly son, Abijah, even as Saul had his Jonathan. We are also surprised to learn that God's way of honoring this lad was to permit him to die of sickness and be buried in a grave! "For he only of Jeroboam shall come to the grave, because in him is found some good thing toward Jehovah, the God of Israel, in the house of Jeroboam" (I Kings 14:13). So horrible was the judgment awaiting the royal family (I Kings 14:10-11) that to avoid it by dying in bed would be a great blessing!

Therefore, Jeroboam's purely pagan plot to deceive the blind old prophet Ahijah by a disguise (like Saul with the witch of

---

[6]It is only in the light of such severe lessons that we can properly explain the episode described in I Kings 20:35-36 (see comments, p. 44).

Endor) not only failed, but became God's means of pronouncing doom upon his dynasty (which ended only two years after his own death) and of unveiling the first frightening suggestion of national deportation to Assyria (I Kings 14:15; cf. Deut. 29:28). Thus ended the reign of the great Kingdom-divider; the great calf-worshipper; the man "who made Israel to sin."[7]

---

[7]For a study of Jeroboam's disastrous confrontation with Abijam of Judah (II Chron. 13), see pp. 29-30.

Chapter 2

THE FIRST SOUTHERN KINGS

Rehoboam (I Kings 12, 14; II Chron. 10–12)

It is probable that Rehoboam's mother was a worshipper of the heathen deity Molech, since she was an Ammonitess (I Kings 14:21; cf. 11:7). Not only so, but she had to compete with seven hundred other "wives" for the affections of an apostate king (I Kings 11:3). Such was the "home life" and the "spiritual environment" in which Rehoboam grew to manhood. Is it any wonder, then, that "he did that which was evil, because he set not his heart to seek Jehovah" (II Chron. 12:14)?

Immediately upon assuming his responsibilities as king, Rehoboam revealed his utter incompetence for this high office (cf. Eccles. 2:18-19). He rejected wise counsel concerning the demands of the northern tribes and followed the proud and immature ideas of "the young men that were grown up with him" (I Kings 12:8).[1] The result, of course, was open rebellion and a permanent split in the kingdom, exactly as God had prophesied through Ahijah (I Kings 12:15; cf. 11:30-35). Barely escaping from Shechem with his life, Rehoboam rallied Judah and Benjamin for a great civil war which was averted only because God intervened. Speaking to the king through Shemaiah the prophet, the Lord explained that the split in the kingdom was neither a chance occurrence, nor a mere human scheme, nor was it accomplished by Satan's power — "this thing is of me" (I Kings 12:24). Not until the nation experiences its great regeneration during the Tribulation will God re-unite the two kingdoms into one (cf. Ezek. 37:15-23).

Somewhat chastened by this sad turn of affairs, Rehoboam followed Jehovah for about three years (II Chron. 11:17). It was at this time that the remnant of true believers in each of the northern tribes began to follow the priests and Levites in the

---

[1]On the question of Rehoboam's age at the death of Solomon, see p. 17.

permanent abandonment of their homes because of Jeroboam's religious revolution (II Chron. 11:13-15; cf. 13:9). Just as the forced exile of hundreds of thousands of godly French Huguenots brought incalculable blessing to surrounding nations in the seventeenth century A.D., so this influx of spiritually-minded Israelites "strengthened the kingdom of Judah and made Rehoboam the son of Solomon strong, three years" (II Chron. 11:17) and modified God's otherwise negative evaluation of his entire reign: "in Judah there were good things found" (II Chron. 12:12).

In a vain and ridiculous attempt to match the glory of Solomon, Rehoboam took eighteen wives (including granddaughters of Jesse, David, and Absalom) and sixty concubines, and begat eighty-eight children (II Chron. 11:18-23). Proud of his harem, building projects, and great prosperity, Rehoboam forsook the Lord. This time, God's instrument of chastening and humiliation was Shishak, king of Egypt, equipped with 1200 chariots, 60,000 horsemen, and countless soldiers (II Chron. 12:1-4).[2] Because of a timely repentance at the preaching of Shemaiah the prophet (I Chron. 12:5; cf. I Kings 12:22), Rehoboam and the kingdom were spared the tragedy of total defeat and subjugation at the hands of the Egyptians. (How the situation had changed since the early days of Solomon when the pharaoh was happy to give his daughter to the king of Israel!) Stripping the temple of all its golden vessels and ornaments symbolized the fact that the glory had already begun to depart. The continuance of the southern kingdom for another three hundred years is a marvellous tribute to the longsuffering of God!

Abijam (I Kings 15:1-8; II Chron. 13)

The author of Kings dismisses Abijam with very few words, none of them encouraging (I Kings 15:1-8). But in II Chroni-

---

[2]Shishak has left to us some references to this campaign on the outside wall of the great temple at Karnak in southern Egypt though he doesn't mention Jerusalem (cf. A.N.E.T., pp. 242 f and 263 f; the map in The Macmillan Bible Atlas, p. 77).

cles 13 we learn of a great victory that God gave to him against Jeroboam of Israel. The victory was unique, not only because of the vast number of Israelites slain (500,000), but also because of the special appeal which Abijam made to the northern enemy and their apostate king (II Chron. 13:4-12). With amazing skill and bitter sarcasm, Abijam exposed the rottenness of Jeroboam's administration which was built upon "worthless men, base fellows" (II Chron. 13:7), and the folly of his man-made religion, propped up by "the golden calves which Jeroboam made you for gods" (II Chron. 13:8) with the sacred offices being staffed by any non-Levite who could pay the price — "a young bullock and seven rams" (II Chron. 13:9)!

In contrast to this hollow sham, said Abijam, we Judeans have the true God, Jehovah, legitimate Aaronic priests, atoning sacrifices, the original table of showbread and the golden candlestick. (How these pointed reminders of happier days and God's ways must have stung the conscience of many a northerner!) Furthermore, declared the bold young king, we have *the ultimate weapon* — "behold, God is with us at our head, and his priests with the trumpets of alarm to sound an alarm against you" (II Chron. 13:12). The magnificent speech ended with a plantive appeal: "O children of Israel, fight ye not against Jehovah, the God of your fathers; for ye shall not prosper."

But even while he pretended to listen to this "summit meeting" oration, Jeroboam was plotting the destruction of his enemies by means of an ambushment. Jehovah, however, had the final word; for through the fervent prayers of godly Judeans and their Jericho-like trumpet blasts and expectant shouts, He brought an unparalleled destruction to Jeroboam's army from which he never recovered (II Chron. 13:20).

We might conclude from all this that Abijam (or Abijah, as the Chronicler calls him) was one of the greatest southern kings. However, the last two verses of this chapter tend to modify our praise and to help us to recognize (especially in the light of I Kings 15:1-8) that Abijam was capable, like his father (cf. II Chron. 11:4, 17; 12:6, 12), of occasional acts of faith in a life of general disobedience to the revealed will of God.

Asa versus Zerah (I Kings 15:9-15; II Chron. 14–15)

Rehoboam and Abijam, two unrighteous but occasionally obedient kings, were followed by Asa and Jehoshaphat, two righteous but occasionally disobedient kings. One great disaster, shared in common by the first three southern kings, was Maacah, a granddaughter of the spoiled and ambitious Absalom. As a sort of Jezebel of Judah, she was Rehoboam's wife, Abijam's mother, and the "Queen Dowager" who held the reins of power in the early days of Asa's administration (the word "mother" in I Kings 15:10 should be translated "grandmother," his own mother presumably having died when he was a child). We are amazed at the boldness of young Asa in deposing Maacah "because she had made an abominable image for an Asherah" (I Kings 15:13). He not only cut down her Asherah, but burned it in the Kidron valley!

The conflict with Baasha described in I Kings 15:16-22 cannot be properly understood apart from some immediately preceding events outlined for us in II Chronicles 14 and 15. Early in Asa's fifteenth year (897 B.C.), God permitted an Ethiopian army (or an Ethiopian-backed Arabian army, judging from the kind of spoils mentioned in II Chron. 14:15) of enormous size to invade Judah. Presumably the peace and prosperity of Asa's early years lulled the people into complacency and pride (note the emphasis on "quiet" and "rest" in II Chron. 14:1, 5, 6, 7), and the nation took its blessings for granted.

Zerah's invasion cured the nation of this problem! On behalf of his people, Asa uttered one of the great prayers of Bible times: "Jehovah, there is none besides thee to help, between the mighty and him that hath no strength: help us, O Jehovah our God; for we rely on thee, and in thy name are we come against this multitude. O Jehovah, thou art our God; let not man prevail against thee" (II Chron. 14:11). With this, "a terror from Jehovah" (II Chron. 14:14, ASV margin) fell upon the enemy and they fled for their very lives. Once again, faith and prayer proved to be the secret and irresistible weapon of God's people, "for the weapons of our warfare are not of the flesh, but mighty before God to the casting down of strongholds" (II Cor. 10:4).

At the moment of victory, the Spirit of God spoke powerfully to Asa through a prophet who appears only once in the Old Testament — Azariah the son of Oded. The message was simple and clear: obedience brings blessing, and disobedience brings defeat (in II Chron. 15:3-6 either Azariah or the Chronicler provided a vivid reminder of the tragedies that stemmed from national disobedience during the days of the judges). The final words had an electrifying effect upon king and people through the Spirit of God: "But be ye strong, and let not your hands be slack; for your work shall be rewarded" (II Chron. 15:7). Hearing this, Asa's enthusiasm for reform and revival was fanned into a white heat. Even northern tribes were affected, and, surprisingly, the tribe of Simeon too, concerning which so little is heard after the time of Joshua (II Chron. 15:9). The resulting influx of believers from the northern tribes into Judah not only alarmed Baasha of Israel (as we shall see), but also provided the necessary dynamic for a spontaneous and widespread revival.

The Great Revival of the third month (the Feast of Weeks?) of Asa's fifteenth year was noteworthy for its intensity and zeal. Not only did the people renew their covenant promises "with a loud voice and with shouting and with trumpets and with cornets," but they determined to kill any man or woman who refused to be revived!

Two important points must be made here. In the first place, Israel was the only nation in history which God ruled through royal and priestly mediators. Therefore, "church and state" were almost a unity, and a religious offense was at the same time a crime against the state! The worship of any other god brought public execution (cf. Exod. 22:20); and even close relatives were responsible for exposing the offender and taking the leading part in his execution (Deut. 13:6-11).

Secondly, the very fact that people who did *not* seek Jehovah were executed proves that regeneration could not have been the prerequisite for "revival" in ancient Israel. Those who *conformed* to the religious regulations of the nation and *avoided* the worship of other deities were accepted as legitimate citizens of the theocracy and were exempt from the penalties of the law. In the Christian dispensation, however, false worship is *never* to be dealt with by physical punishment (I Cor. 5:12-13), and "revival" can *only* occur in the hearts of *regenerated* people (cf. II Cor. 13:5). Having made this distinction, we must also recognize that God's desire for Israel was always individual regeneration first of all (Ezek. 36:27), and then revival of *heart-religion* (Deut. 10:16; Jer. 4:4). Thus, Isaiah (1:10-20), Micah (6:6-8), and Hosea (6:6) all denounced mere outward conformity to ceremonial requirements without a corresponding revival of the heart.

Asa versus Baasha (I Kings 15:16-22; II Chron. 16)

Second Chronicles 15 ends with a summary statement about the peacefulness of the early years of Asa's reign (cf. 14:6). The correct translation of II Chronicles 15:19 is: "there was no war unto the five and thirtieth year of the reign of Asa" (instead of "no more war" as in ASV). But we know that Zerah's invasion occurred in his fifteenth year (II Chron. 15:10). Therefore, the Chronicler must be measuring these years from the division of the kingdom in 931 B.C., for the 15th year of Asa's own reign was also the 35th year of the divided kingdom. Such an interpretation, strange though it may seem at first glance, actually solves two chronological problems of considerable importance. First, it eliminates the anomaly of Baasha waiting twenty-one years to block the southward flow of his citizens (II Chron. 15:9; 16:1). Second, and more important, it eliminates the absurdity of Baasha invading Judah nine years after he had died! (cf. I Kings 15:33).[3]

Thus, Baasha's invasion of Judah and his fortification of Ramah (five miles north of Jerusalem) was his Berlin wall response to the powerful magnet of revival in Jerusalem to the south (cf. II Chron. 15:9). The king of Israel realized full well that it was his most stalwart citizens who were leaving him, the very life blood of the nation, and he took drastic means to stop it.

Asa panicked when he saw this happening. Instead of trusting the Lord, as he had done only a few months earlier when

---

[3]For a full discussion of this and other chronological problems during the period of the Divided Kingdom, see Edwin R. Thiele, *The Mysterious Numbers of the Hebrew Kings* (Grand Rapids: Wm. B. Eerdmans Publishing Co., 1965), pp. 59 f.

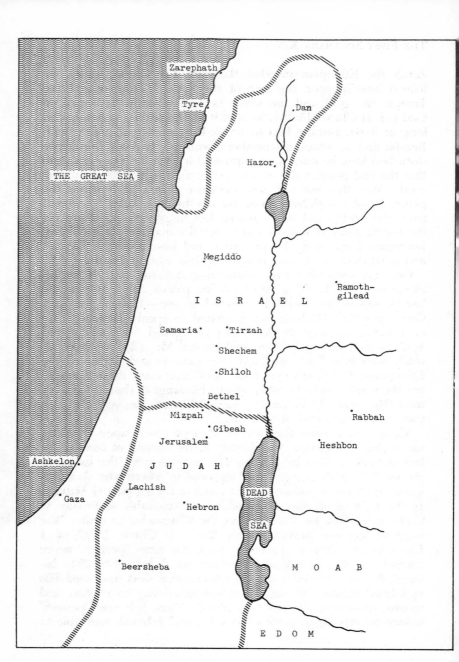

3. The Kingdoms of Israel and Judah

Zerah the Ethiopian invaded the land (II Chron. 14:9), he leaned heavily upon the arm of the flesh. Taking out of the Temple the gold and the silver he had recently dedicated to God (cf. II Chron. 15:18), he sent it to Damascus, to Ben-hadad king of Syria, bribing him to break his commercial treaty with Baasha and to attack his northern borders. If Asa's conscience disturbed him, he must have supressed it with the rationalization that the end justifies the means. After all, did not the plan succeed? Was this not sufficient evidence that God honored the plan? Baasha withdrew from Ramah to cope with the threat from the north, and Asa commanded his people to dismantle the fortifications at Ramah and to use the materials to build two fortresses, Geba and Mizpah, three and four miles to the east and northwest, as his own defense system against Baasha.

One day soon after this, while congratulating himself for his cleverness, Asa heard a knock on his palace door. It was the last person in the world he wanted to see — Hanani the seer, God's prophet! Without being invited to speak, Hanani delivered God's message to Asa: (1) you could have conquered Syria as well as Israel if you had trusted Me; (2) you have already seen how God answered your prayers and destroyed the Ethiopians; (3) God's eyes have "legs" that carry them throughout the whole world to bring special blessings to those who truly trust Him; and (4) because of your deliberate sin, you will have wars to the very end of your reign.

These words from the God of Heaven came upon the king like a clap of thunder. Completely losing control of himself, he lashed back at God by putting His prophet into "the house of the stocks" (ASV margin) and oppressing others who dared to question his royal policies or who came to the support of Hanani. In the light of all this, it is indeed a remarkable testimony to God's grace that He could direct the Chronicler to write: "the heart of Asa was perfect all his days" (II Chron. 15:17; cf. I Kings 15:14). When applied to men, the term "perfect" never carried the idea of sinless perfection (cf. I John 1:8, 10). Instead, it characterized a person who trusted God and used His appointed means (through Levitical sacrifices) to confess and receive atonement for sins committed. Thus, Job was "perfect" before he was even tested (Job 1:1), and Jehovah was able to say of David that he "kept my commandments, and followed me with all his heart, to do that only which was right in my eyes" (I Kings 14:8), even though he was guilty of some horrible crimes. The only *absolutely* perfect man who ever lived was our Lord Jesus Christ.

Asa not only outlived Baasha, but also Omri, the founder of a dynasty of fanatical Baal-worshippers (see Chap. 3). Toward the end of his reign, which came twenty-seven years after the revival and the defeat of Baasha, Asa must have turned away from God again. As a result, he was smitten with a great and loathsome disease in his feet. Instead of turning to God and His prophets, he turned to pagan (foreign?) physicians who were probably little more than witch-doctors. Two years later he died and was buried in a bed filled with sweet spices and surrounded with incense burners (cf. Jer. 34:5). Thus ended the long reign of the godliest king to sit on the throne of Judah until Hezekiah and Josiah.

Jehoshaphat (II Chron. 17–20)

The character and reign of Jehoshaphat constitute a fascinating study in contrasts. On the one hand, some of his spiritual attainments were almost without parallel in the history of the kingdom. But on the other hand, he repeatedly and flagrantly involved himself and his people in alliances with the husband and two sons of wicked Queen Jezebel. Thus, by his refusal to exercise spiritual discernment with regard to the utter apostasy of Israel, he practically cancelled the spiritual benefits that came from his reforms in Judah. The application of this lesson to the ecumenical pressures which pastors of fundamental churches must face in our own day is quite obvious.

Jehoshaphat's reign began impressively. He was *against* Israel (II Chron. 17:1), and "he walked in the first ways of his father David" (II Chron. 17:3 — an intentional contrast to the post-Bathsheba phase of David's career). Even more impressive is the record of Bible-teaching teams, consisting of princes as well as priests and Levites, "who taught in Judah, having the book of the law of Jehovah with them; and they went about throughout all the cities of Judah, and taught among the people" (II Chron. 17:9). As a result, God gave him such honor and prestige that even the Philistines and Arabians brought tribute (II Chron. 17:11).

Approximately half way through his twenty-five year reign, however, Jehoshaphat made a decision that in later years almost brought his kingdom and the Davidic dynasty to destruction: "he joined affinity with Ahab" (II Chron. 18:1) by accepting the pagan Athaliah, daughter of Ahab and Jezebel, as his son's wife. The alliance became so strong through this marriage that Jehoshaphat really had no choice when Ahab urged him to join in a battle against Ramoth-gilead.[4] Barely escaping with his life, Jehoshaphat returned to Jerusalem only to receive a scathing denunciation from God through the prophet Jehu (II Chron. 19:2). It was at this time that his son Jehoram became the co-regent.[5]

Now Jehoshaphat launched a new series of reforms in Judah "and brought them back unto Jehovah, the God of their fathers" (II Chron. 19:4). Judges were appointed in all fortified cities, and were admonished to do their work as unto the Lord, avoiding all bribes (vss. 4-11). This was just what was needed to face the next crisis — an invasion of Moabites and Ammonites from the east. Gathering the nation before the Temple court, the king prayed a prayer of faith and of child-like trust in Jehovah. The remarkable response from heaven came through a Levite named Jehaziel: "Fear ye not, neither be dismayed by reason of this great multitude: for the battle is not yours, but God's. . . . ye shall not need to fight this battle: set yourselves, stand ye still, and see the salvation of Jehovah with you . . ." (II Chron. 20:14-17; cf. Exod. 14:13-14). The victory was total, the spoils were enormous, and "the fear of God was on all . . . countries, when they heard that Jehovah fought against the enemies of Israel" (II Chron. 20:29).

In spite of all these blessings, and in spite of his tragic experience with Ahab, Jehoshaphat joined with wicked Ahaziah of Israel in a shipbuilding project at Ezion-geber. The Lord denounced this alliance through the prophet Eliezer and destroyed the ships (II Chron. 20:35-37). Even worse, his son Jehoram,

---

[4]For a discussion of this battle and Jehoshaphat's part in it, see pp. 45-48.
[5]Edwin R. Thiele discusses the chronology of this period in *The Mysterious Numbers of the Hebrew Kings*, pp. 64-71.

upon becoming co-regent, murdered his six younger brothers and some of the princes (II Chron. 21:4). As a result, Jehoram received a letter from Elijah the prophet denouncing him and predicting a horrible death (21:12-15). Still refusing to learn the lesson of separation from apostasy, Jehoshaphat joined himself and his army to Jehoram of Israel in an expedition against Moab (II Kings 3:4-7). It was only by the grace of God, through Elisha's special intercession on behalf of Jehoshaphat (in spite of the presence of Jehoram) that both armies were spared a total catastrophe (II Kings 3:8-15).[6]

Thus, Jehoshaphat made his mark in Judah's history as a king who did "that which was right in the eyes of Jehovah" (I Kings 22:43); but appended to this official evaluation of his reign were these tragic words in red ink: "And Jehoshaphat made peace with the king of Israel" (I Kings 22:44). May God help us to keep our record of Christian life and service pure and clean by "cleansing ourselves from all defilement of flesh and spirit, perfecting holiness in the fear of God" (II Cor. 7:1).

---

[6]See pp. 69, 71, for a study of this battle.

4. View of the hill of Samaria where Omri established his capital after abandoning Tirzah. Courtesy, Matson Photo Service.

Chapter 3

OMRI AND AHAB — DYNASTY OF BAAL

The Dynasty Established (I Kings 16:15-34)

Omri was founder of the fourth dynasty in the Kingdom of Israel. Jeroboam and Baasha were founders of the first two dynasties, but they were each followed by sons who reigned only two years. The third dynasty hardly deserves such a title, for it only lasted a week! Zimri, who had murdered Baasha's son, himself died in a siege seven days later when Omri, captain of the army, attacked him in the capital city of Tirzah. Within five years, Omri crushed a rival to the throne (Tibni) and greatly strengthened the kingdom by purchasing a strategic hill called Samaria (see Fig. 4) and building a new, well-fortified capital there. So important was this move from an international standpoint that for over a hundred years the Assyrians called Israel "the land of Omri."[1]

Omri's other claim to fame (or rather, infamy), was the sealing of an alliance with Phoenicia through the marriage of his son Ahab to Jezebel, daughter of Ethbaal, King of the Sidonians. To make Jezebel feel perfectly at home, Ahab erected a temple for Baal in Samaria, thus officially abandoning the compromise calf-cult of Jeroboam. Possibly he appealed to the example of Solomon who had encouraged his foreign wives by erecting pagan shrines for them around Jerusalem (I Kings 11:7).

As a measure of the wickedness of the new dynasty, a prominent citizen of Bethel publicly defied the curse of Joshua upon Jericho. Joshua had not prohibited all future settlement in this city, but only its *fortification* (Josh. 6:26 — "gates"), for it was inhabited again not long after his day (Judges 3:13). It is true that God's warnings of coming judgment may lie dormant for many centuries, but they dare not be lightly defied or challenged. So Hiel's presumption cost him two of his sons, and the entire nation must have been stunned by this spectacular dem-

---

[1]Pritchard, *ANET*, pp. 284, 285.

onstration that God will fulfill his promise: "I watch over my word to perform it" (Jer. 1:12).

Ahab and Benhadad (I Kings 20)

But this was only a mild warning from Jehovah. The next blow was a three-year drought followed by the slaughter of 450 prophets of Baal at the hand of Elijah.[2] But still the message did not get through to the sinful heart of Ahab. Therefore another disaster loomed over the horizon in the person of Ben-

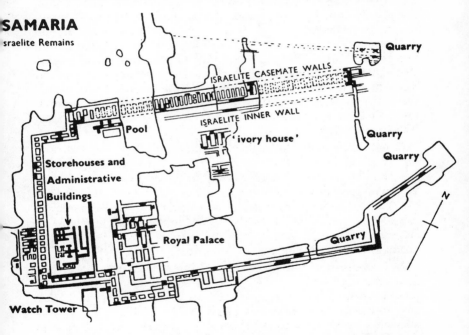

5. Plans of Samaria, capital of Israel, with its stout casemate defense walls, royal palace and House of Ivory. Courtesy, Inter-Varsity Fellowship.

---

[2]See discussion in Chapter 4.

hadad, King of Syria (I Kings 20:1), who laid siege to Samaria. Realizing that he had overextended his supply lines, Benhadad tried to strike a bargain with Ahab: "Thy silver and thy gold are mine; thy wives also and thy children, even the goodliest, are mine" (I Kings 20:3). When Ahab quickly accepted these terms (including the loss of Jezebel!), the greedy king demanded even more and thus lost everything, being foiled by his own clumsy frankness. Wicked though he was, Ahab was not totally devoid of the courage of a king. To Benhadad's ridiculous boasting, Ahab replied with calm dignity, "Let not him that girdeth on his armor boast himself as he that putteth it off" (I Kings 20:11).

Ahab was still King of Israel, in spite of his spiritual blindness, and God honored him to the extent of speaking encouraging words to him through a prophet on three different occasions (I Kings 20:13, 22, 28). Benhadad was overconfident. He and his thirty-two kings were drunk in their tents and therefore hardly knew what hit them. Blaming the slaughter of their soldiers on a theological miscalculation (I Kings 20:23), the Syrians attacked again and failed even more disastrously (I Kings 20:29, 30), the reason being theological rather than military (I Kings 20:28).

It is important to recognize that *all* of Israel's military victories were won by obeying the Lord. Of no other nation can such a statement be made. Joshua prevailed against Amalek only when Moses' arms were held high in prayer (Exod. 17:8-15). His attack on Ai failed because of Achan's sin (Josh. 7). God cut down Gideon's army to a mere 300 in order that he would not trust in the arm of the flesh (Judges 7:2). In fact, if Israel really trusted in the Lord only one soldier would be sufficient to chase 1,000 and two could put 10,000 to flight (Deut. 32:30). Zechariah tells us that at the close of Israel's tribulation period "He that is feeble among them at that day shall be as David; and the house of David shall be as God, as the angel of Jehovah before them" (12:8). For us, too, "though we walk in the flesh, we do not war according to the flesh" (II Cor. 10:3). In fact, said the great apostle, "I glory in my weaknesses, that the power of Christ may rest upon me. Wherefore I take pleasure in weaknesses . . . for Christ's sake: for when I am weak, then am I strong" (II Cor. 12:9-10).

Ahab made the fatal mistake of assuming, in the hour of Benhadad's humiliation, that *he*, not Jehovah, could dictate the terms. Instead of executing God's enemy, Ahab, like Saul before him (I Sam. 15:9), decided to spare the captive king and accomplish his own purposes through him. Apparently he wanted a strong kingdom in Damascus to serve as a buffer between Israel and Assyria, instead of trusting Jehovah to be his wall of defense (cf. Isa. 26:1). Also, there would be the privilege of having Israelite bazaars in the very important commercial center of Damascus (I Kings 20:34). Outwardly impressive, the plan was actually nearsighted and cruel, for Ahab not only had to take his army to fight the Assyrian king, Shalmaneser III, at Qarqar along with other western kings (853 B.C.), but shortly thereafter had to lead his weary army against Benhadad, the very king he had just pardoned. This not only cost him his life but the lives of many of his men.

6. Assyrian battle scene. The royal chariot with three occupants is protected by soldiers armed with bows and daggers. From relief of Ashurnasirpal II at Nimrud. Courtesy, Inter-Varsity Fellowship.

God's method of exposing Ahab's blunder is fascinating. An unnamed "son of the prophets" was instructed by God to get wounded at the hand of a fellow prophet and then deliver a message of doom to the king through his head bandages. The first prophet refused (not surprisingly!), and was therefore killed by a lion on the highway. What severe discipline for the preparation for God's representatives! We *must* assume that this young prophet, like all true believers, had the God-given capacity to discern the voice of God (John 10:27, I John 4:1), and, therefore, like the unnamed prophet from Judah who suffered an identical fate (I Kings 13:24), was guilty of elevating his personal desires above the known will of God (cf. the experience of Jonah). A second prophet cooperated with this strange command, sorely wounding his friend, and the king received the message of God in such a forceful way that "He went to his house heavy and displeased" (I Kings 20:43).

Naboth's Vineyard (I Kings 21)

This, of course, is the background to the tragedy of Naboth's vineyard. Morose and disconsolate, the childish king wanted a new toy with which to play. When his whim was thwarted, he sulked homeward "heavy and displeased" (cf. I Kings 20:43), and pouted on his dining room couch. When Jezebel asked for an explanation, he gave only a partial answer. Naboth had said, "Jehovah forbid it me, that I should give the inheritance of my fathers unto thee" (I Kings 21:3). The Lord had prohibited the outright and perpetual sale of any inherited property to someone who was not in the immediate family (Lev. 25:23; cf. Micah 2:1, 2) because the land belonged to *Jehovah* and had been given to the families of Israel as a foretaste of blessings and privileges (Micah 4:4).

Ahab knew, of course, that Jezebel would laugh at such a law. Amazed that a *king* would accept "no" for an answer, she proceeded to do what any Phoenician ruler would do under such circumstances: simply destroy the uncooperative citizen.[3] Jeze-

---

[3]Years before, Samuel had warned Israel that land-grabbing would be the typical policy of kings (I Sam. 8:14).

bel was careful, however, to honor Jewish law to the extent of obtaining *two* witnesses (Deut. 17:6) and a legitimate accusation (cf. Lev. 24:16). The mock trial is a painful reminder of what our blessed Lord experienced at the hands of men who were even more guilty than Jezebel (Matt. 26:59-67; 23:32-36; I Thess. 2:14-16). Naboth's sons were stoned too (II Kings 9:26), and thus the property had no heir. As Ahab went to possess it, his chariot was followed by two officers, Jehu and Bidkar, who later recalled this vivid scene and helped to fulfill Elijah's terrible judgment (II Kings 9:25). So Naboth's blood (like that of Abel — Heb. 12:24) cried out to God, even while being licked up by scavenger dogs, and God heard that cry (I Kings 21:19).[4]

Ahab's Last Battle (I Kings 22)

Jehoshaphat, the King of Judah, was partly responsible for the disastrous campaign against Ramoth-Gilead, for he had "joined affinity with Ahab" (II Chron. 18:1) by marrying his son Jehoram to Athaliah, daughter of Ahab and Jezebel (II Chron. 21:6; 22: 2, 3) at least ten years earlier (cf. II Kings 8:17 with 26). So when Ahab celebrated this reunion with his southern relatives by providing a huge banquet (II Chron. 18:2), Jehoshaphat was really in no position to deny Ahab's urgent request to help him recapture the border town of Ramoth-Gilead from the hands of the Syrians. Ahab was especially anxious for the battle, because Benhadad had betrayed his covenant of three years earlier (I Kings 20:34) in taking this trans-Jordan territory from Israel. What Jehoshaphat expected to gain from such a campaign is not at all clear.

Having already decided to go to battle with Ahab, Jehoshaphat now decided to inquire of Jehovah. It was somewhat late for this, but his insistence on hearing from a genuine prophet of Jehovah (I Kings 22:7, 8) was doubtless the very factor that saved his life in the battle. Ahab, having anticipated such a request, had trained four hundred men to imitate the prophets of Jehovah (were these formerly Jezebel's 400 prophets of the Asherah?), being careful to use Jehovah's name (I Kings 22:

4See pp. 62-63 for an analysis of Elijah's confrontation with Ahab at Naboth's vineyard (I Kings 21:17-29).

11, 12, 24). One of them, a certain Zedekiah, even made horns
of iron to match the vivid imagery of Moses' final blessing upon
the Joseph tribes: "his horns are as the horns of the wild ox:
with them he shall push the peoples, all of them, even the ends
of the earth" (Deut. 33:17). This was apparently sufficient to
convince Jehoshaphat in spite of all that Micaiah, the 401st
prophet, could say.

Micaiah, the son of Imlah, was truly one of God's great ones.
His testimony stood out if for no other reason than that Ahab
hated him (I Kings 22:8). The king, with itching ears, was
anxious to hear his own desires echoed by the mouths of his
well-trained prophets (II Tim. 4:3), but here was one who remained utterly aloof from the superimposed ecumenism of the
new state religion. He was urged to conform his words to theirs
and thus to rubber-stamp the king's plan. At first glance, it would
seem that Micaiah succumbed to the pressure (I Kings 22:15),
but Ahab's angry response shows clearly that Micaiah's tone of
voice intentionally betrayed the insincerity of his words. Then
came the straight message, at the king's own request: Israel
would be defeated and Ahab would die (cf. Samuel's message to
Saul at Endor — I Sam. 28:19).

God confirmed the judgment with a parabolic vision, which
explained in story form the complete sovereignty of God in
manipulating the evil devices of men. If the king and his false
prophets thought they could control the outcome of battles and
even their own destiny by purely magical means, the truth of the
matter was that they, like Satan their master, were under *God's*
control (cf. Gen. 50:20; Ps. 76:10; Dan. 4:17), having willfully
sold themselves to sin's dominion (cf. I Kings 21:20). In the
vision, the spirit who volunteered to entice Ahab's prophets may
have been a personification of the spirit of false prophecy, as in
Zechariah 13:2 (cf. I John 4:6). God had given up these wicked
men to judicial hardening, and their doom was sealed (cf. Rom.
1:24-32), as exemplified by the blasphemous response of Zedekiah and God's personal judgment upon him (I Kings 22:24, 25).

The last recorded appeal of Micaiah as he was dragged off
to prison ("Hear, ye peoples, all of you" — I Kings 22:28b), may
not have turned the two kings from their course of action but
in the marvelous providence of God it found lodgment in the

hearts of two parents a hundred years later who named their son in his honor: Micah. It is significant that Micah's first recorded words were the final ones of his namesake: "Hear, ye peoples, all of you" (Micah 1:2). No one can fully measure the impact of one godly life upon the hearts of other men, but God assures us that it is great (Dan. 12:3).

Ahab's determination to disguise himself during the battle reveals two facts: (1) he was essentially pagan in his concept of God's knowledge; and (2) his death was even more obviously the work of God. The enemy did not recognize him, but "a certain man drew his bow at a venture, and smote the king of Israel between the joints of his armor" (I Kings 22:34). The Achilles' Heel of Ahab was not the crack in his armor but his willful rebellion against God. And once a man has made God his enemy there can be no escape: "though they hide themselves in the top of Carmel, I will search and take them out thence; and though they be hid from my sight in the bottom of the sea, thence will I command the serpent, and it shall bite them . . . and I will set mine eyes upon them for evil, and not for good" (Amos 9:3, 4).

Fatally wounded, Ahab bravely held himself up in his chariot to encourage his men, and died as the sun set. It was not his magnificent ivory-inlaid palace of Samaria (I Kings 22:39) that welcomed him home this time, but the same dogs that licked the blood of Naboth. And so God clearly vindicated his faithful prophet Micaiah, who had staked his claim to the true prophetic office on the certainty of this event: "If thou return at all in peace, Jehovah hath not spoken by me" (I Kings 22:28).

It is hard not to be astounded at the stupidity of Jehoshaphat. Rushing into the battle with his royal robes flowing in the wind, he was a perfect target for the enemy. King Benhadad commanded his men to concentrate on Ahab, for whom he had no love in spite of great mercy previously received (I Kings 20:34). Thinking he was the King of Israel, the Syrian captains pursued after the defenseless and desperate Jehoshaphat. Whatever armor he may have had was useless, but he "cried out" to Jehovah in one of the most famous "foxhole prayers" of Bible history. "And Jehovah helped him; and God moved them to depart from him" (II Chron. 18:31), because in spite of his inconsistencies and compromises he basically had done "that which is right in the eyes of Jehovah" (I Kings 22:43; II Chron. 19:3).

It is true that God spared his life, but upon his return to Jerusalem Jehoshaphat was severely rebuked by Hanani, the seer, in words which are rich in warning to Christians today who feel that the Lord's work can best be promoted by cooperation with unregenerate religious leaders: "Shouldest thou help the wicked and love them that hate Jehovah? for this thing wrath is upon thee from before Jehovah" (II Chron. 19:2). To this, we may add the words of the Apostle Paul: "Be not unequally yoked with unbelievers: for what fellowship have righteousness and iniquity? or what communion hath light with darkness . . . or what portion hath a believer with an unbeliever?" (II Cor. 6:14-15).

The Destruction of Ahab's Dynasty

When King Ahab permitted his wife Jezebel to kill Naboth for the sake of obtaining his vineyard, God sent Elijah to denounce him for his sin. Among other things, Elijah said: "Behold, I will bring evil upon thee, and will utterly sweep thee away, and will cut off from Ahab every man child" (I Kings 21:21). In startling fulfillment of this grim prophecy, the following judgments fell upon Ahab's family:

(1) Ahab himself was slain by an enemy arrow, in spite of every effort to disguise himself (I Kings 22:34).

(2) Ahab's son Ahaziah died childless after a fall in his palace (II Kings 1:1-17).

(3) Jehoram, Ahab's second son and Ahaziah of Judah, his grandson, were killed by Jehu (II Kings 9:24).

(4) Ahab's wife, Jezebel, was likewise killed by Jehu (II Kings 9:33).

(5) Ahab's seventy sons (by various concubines) were beheaded by the elders of Israel at the command of Jehu (II Kings 10:1-10).

(6) Jehoram of Judah, son-in-law of Ahab, lost all of his wives and sons except Athaliah, their son Ahaziah, and a daughter, Jehosheba (II Chron. 21:17).

(7) Jehoram himself died of a horrible disease (II Chron. 21:19).

(8) Some of Jehoram's male relatives and descendants were killed by Jehu (II Kings 10:13; II Chron. 22:8).

(9) All the rest of his male relatives and descendants were killed by Athaliah herself, with the exception of Joash (II Chron. 22:10).

(10) While she reigned in Judah (841-835 B.C.), Athaliah was the *only* living representative of Ahab's family besides her daughter Jehosheba and her little son, Joash, who was also the *only* male representative of David's line. Thus, when Athaliah was finally slain (II Kings 11:16; II Chron. 23:15), the amazing prophecy of Elijah was fulfilled; for both Jehosheba and Joash were led into Jehovah's spiritual family by the high priest Jehoiada, the husband of Jehosheba and the foster-father of Joash (II Chron. 22:10-12).

"He that being often reproved hardeneth his neck shall suddenly be destroyed, and that without remedy" (Prov. 29:1). "It is a fearful thing to fall into the hands of the living God" (Heb. 10:31).

Chapter 4

ELIJAH: FROM THE BROOK CHERITH TO THE JUNIPER TREE

The Appearing of Elijah (I Kings 17:1)

Like a meteor suddenly flashing across the darkened sky, Elijah appears on the scene without genealogy, without historical background, and without warning. One thunderous judgment from heaven through his lips and he disappeared without a trace — "As Jehovah, the God of Israel, liveth, before whom I stand, there shall not be dew nor rain these years, but according to my word" (I Kings 17:1).

God permitted neither debate nor dialogue between His prophet and Ahab, the apostate king of Israel (compare Elisha's attitude toward Ahab's son, Jehoram — II Kings 3:14). The king was left to stagger for three more years under the colossal judgment of an unrelieved drought, six months of it having been experienced already (compare I Kings 18:1 with Luke 4:25 and James 5:17). Not that the nation had no warning at all. Centuries before, Moses had said that national apostasy would cause the rains to cease (Deut. 11:17; 28:24). And now that Jehovah had been officially repudiated, His providential blessings upon this land came to an end.

Elijah and the Ravens (I Kings 17:2-7)

To prevent His prophet from being besieged by the desperate entreaties of the dying and the dire threats of Ahab and Jezebel (who doubtless concluded that it was the magical power of Elijah rather than Jehovah that had cast this evil spell upon their land), the Lord whisked him away to a secluded spot just east of the Jordan in the rugged hill country of Gilead. We may also assume that Elijah himself needed this time of retreat and this spectacular reminder that God alone was his source of supply and strength. As the ravens fed him each morning and evening, Elijah was made aware of the basically supernatural character

50

of his ministry in a day of desperate spiritual darkness when Israel stood at the crossroads of her destiny. So titanic was this struggle that Elijah on at least one later occasion needed to be fed by God again under a juniper tree through angelic agency (I Kings 19:5).

Elijah and the Widow of Zarephath (I Kings 17:8-23)

And yet, even this miraculous supply had its God-appointed limitations. When the brook dried up, no supernatural fountain appeared. Elijah was now commanded to proceed to Zarephath, a Phoenician coastal town (the modern Sarafand) between Tyre and Sidon. It was not that there were no widows in Israel who could help him. The Lord Jesus explained (Luke 4:25) that in His sovereign grace God chose a woman who, though a believer in Jehovah, was not even an Israelite, in order to rebuke the utter apostasy of His people (see a similar rebuke in Matt. 8:10 — "I have not found so great faith, no, not in Israel"). Furthermore, it was a special rebuke to Queen Jezebel, for she never dreamed that Elijah would be hiding in her own homeland (I Kings 18:10)!

The widow of Zarephath was subjected to a very severe test of faith and she passed it. When Elijah challenged her to give him the last morsel of food, "she went and did according to the saying of Elijah" and was richly blessed for her obedience. Our Lord later enunciated this principle: "Seek ye first his kingdom and his righteousness, and all these things shall be added unto you" (Matt. 6:33).

Her final test was to trust Elijah's God concerning her dead son. It was not "to bring her sin to remembrance" (I Kings 17:18) that God permitted this to happen (she still clung to the popular superstition that the proximity of a prophet enabled God to see one's sins more clearly — a superstition that has not completely died even in our day!). Rather, God allowed this tragedy to occur in order that He might be glorified through it (cf. John 9:3). Great is the mystery of God's providential purposes! As God's instrument for bringing this boy back to mortal life, Elijah became a true forerunner of the Lord Jesus Christ (see p. 75, for comparisons with the work of Elijah and Christ).

The widow not only received back her son, but also regained her confidence that her remarkable guest was indeed God's man.

The Prophets of Jehovah (I Kings 18:4, 13)

By the third year after the miracle of the widow's son, the drought had taken its devastating toll in the land. Whatever the fate of the people might have been, Ahab was desperately concerned about his horses, for they were his first line of military defense (I Kings 5).[1] A few years after this drought in the year 853 B.C., the Assyrian king, Shalmaneser III, informs us that Ahab appeared at Qarqar in Syria with 2,000 chariots; so his efforts to save his horses must not have been totally unsuccessful.[2]

7. Ruins of horse stables with hitching posts and mangers, probably from the period of Ahab, at Megiddo. Courtesy, Oriental Institute.

[1]See Figure 7. These ruins of horse stables at Megiddo very likely date to the reign of Ahab.

[2]Cf. Pritchard, *ANET*, p. 279.

The rainless skies were not caused by Elijah's magical powers as Ahab and Jezebel thought ("Is it thou, thou troubler of Israel?" I Kings 18:17; cf. Josh. 7:25 concerning Achan), but by their own persecution of the prophets of Jehovah (I Kings 18:4) and replacement with 850 Baal and Asherah prophets imported from Phoenicia and supported from the royal treasury (I Kings 18:19). The one hundred surviving "prophets of Jehovah" were probably the same as the "sons of the prophets" who knew of Elijah's forthcoming translation to heaven (II Kings 2:3, 5). They may even have traced their heritage back to the prophetic guilds of Samuel's day (I Sam. 19:20). But Elijah must not have considered their testimony to be very outstanding; for in spite of the fact that Obadiah had saved a hundred of them alive in caves (there are about 2,000 caves in Mt. Carmel alone), Elijah still insisted that "I, even I only, am left a prophet of Jehovah" (I Kings 18:22). The Lord corrected this statement by assuring him that seven thousand had not bowed the knee to Baal (I Kings 19:18). Nevertheless, it must be admitted that if these one hundred prophets were the nucleus of the prophetic schools at Bethel and Jericho (II Kings 2:3, 5), they were in great need of systematic instruction in the things of God (cf. II Kings 2: 15-18).

Elijah on Mount Carmel (I Kings 18:19-39)

The contest on Mt. Carmel was a spectacular vindication of the uniqueness and sovereignty of Jehovah in a day of satanic darkness. Never in all history was the point more clearly made that "no idol is anything in the world and there is no God but one" (I Cor. 8:4). The three-and-one-half-year famine had doubtless shaken the confidence of many in the ability of Baal, the god of fertility, to answer their prayers. But if any yet hesitated, Elijah's demonstration would remove every excuse for following this vile system of worship.

The issue was crystal clear: "If Jehovah be God, follow him; but if Baal, then follow him" (I Kings 18:21). God has never tolerated middle-of-the-road, lukewarm compromises in spiritual matters. The Lord Jesus warned the church of Laodicea with these words: "I know thy works, that thou art neither cold nor hot: I would that thou wert cold or hot. So because thou art lukewarm, and neither hot nor cold, I will spew thee out of my mouth" (Rev. 3:15, 16). These words certainly do not mean that God does not care whether people believe Him or not; but they do mean that nothing can be quite so dangerous to the spiritual vitality of a church or nation as the presence and prominence of those who profess to know God but by their works deny Him (Titus 1:16). The church of Jesus Christ today would be enormously strengthened if all those who profess to be its friends, but who secretly deny the authority of its Lord, would depart from it. A mixed multitude can only bring compromise and spiritual defeat to God's people.

Elijah gave every possible advantage to the 450 prophets of Baal (did Jezebel's 400 prophets of the Asherah stay home as a "back-up team"?). He not only permitted himself to be outnumbered four hundred and fifty to one, but also chose a prominent hill near the Baal centers of Phoenicia where the power of this deity would presumably be greater. He gave them the privilege of choosing the best bullock, and of having most of the day to exercise their skills in evoking a response from their great god. All the people (including representatives from all twelve tribes — I Kings 18:19, 20) agreed that the contest was a fair one (I Kings 18:24), though Jezebel's absence may suggest her deep misgivings about such a contest.

Elijah's analysis of the plight of the Baal prophets is instructive. That there was a humorous aspect to the whole episode is undeniable, and Elijah was God's spokesman in pointing this out (for a similar exposure of the utter folly of idolatry, see Isa. 44: 9-20). The evils of idolatry are twofold: (1) it involves a forsaking of nature's testimony to the conscience that only one true God can exist; and (2) it pictures God (or the gods) in terms of human sin and frailty (compare the double denunciation in Jer. 2:13). In the light of such religious irrationality on the part of God-created minds and hearts, it is understandable that "He that sitteth in the heavens shall laugh . . ." (Ps. 2:4). So Elijah taunted these desperate men in their well-deserved hour of public humiliation: "Cry aloud; for he is a god: either he is musing, or he is gone aside [a euphemistic expression], or he is on a journey, or peradventure he sleepeth and must be awaked!"

We, too, must laugh at such a concept of deity. For we have a God whose presence permeates and penetrates the highest heaven, the lowest Sheol, and the uttermost part of the sea (Ps. 139:8, 9). Not only can He be contacted, but He is inescapable, for He fills both heaven and earth (Jer. 23:24). And as for alertness to the cries of His people, "he that keepeth Israel will neither slumber nor sleep" (Ps. 121:4). So accustomed are we to hearing such truths that we tend to take them for granted. But the otherwise clever and clear-thinking Greeks, unenlightened by the Word of God, populated Mt. Olympus with just such projections of their sinful imaginations concerning the God who created them (cf. Acts 17:16, 29). Only if God condescends to reveal Himself to men in a special way can they grasp anything of His true character.

But, there was also a tragic side to this great summit meeting. Hundreds of men who had devoted their lives to promoting the cult of Baal now sank to the desperate expedient of slashing their own bodies with knives in order to provoke their god to respond, if for no other reason, then at least out of sympathy for their physical agonies. Jehovah had long since warned His people against doing such things (Lev. 19:28; Deut. 14:1), not only because the body is sacred (I Cor. 6:19, ASV), but because human efforts and sacrifices apart from faith in God's revealed will are utterly worthless (cf. Micah 6:6-8). And so it is today — millions are destroying their lives and even their eternal destinies out of loyalty to such gods as materialism and blind evolutionism (to say nothing of the gods of false cults and religions), which can neither save men's souls nor even answer their prayers.

The calm assurance and dignity of Elijah provides a startling contrast to the heated frenzy of the pagan prophets. Gathering the people, he quickly rebuilt the local Jehovah altar (apparently tolerated by the Lord because Jerusalem was now inaccessible to His northern worshippers — I Kings 19:10, Romans 11: 3; cf. II Chron. 16:1) that had been thrown down by Baal's worshippers. Drenched with twelve jars of sea water, and with only one man of like passions with us (James 5:17) to offer a short prayer on its behalf, this second-choice bullock (I Kings 18:23) seemed a poor candidate for heavenly acceptance. But the great difference lay in the fact that Elijah's God *actually existed* and that Elijah was *His servant!*

That Jehovah could *answer by fire* had already been demonstrated in spectacular ways to Abraham (Gen. 15:17), Lot (Gen. 19:24), Aaron's sons (Lev. 10:2), and Solomon (II Chron. 7:1). No mere lightning bolt was this; for stones, dust, and even the sea water all vanished, along with the bullock and the wood. Truly "our God is a consuming fire" (Deut. 4:24; Heb. 12:29) — and may all mankind take heed!

Ridiculous beyond expression is the modern liberal suggestion that "Elijah poured naphtha, which he obtained from a nearby source, on the altar and that he used a magnifying lens to focus the sun's rays and ignite the fire."[3] It is "Christian rationalists" such as this who would explain Jesus' walk upon the sea in terms of a shallow sand bar, or the feeding of the five thousand as an emotional response of the crowd to a boy's willingness to share his lunch, so that they all spontaneously took out the lunches they had selfishly hidden in their garments! Church members of some denominations would be surprised to learn how many such men occupy positions of great influence in their church-supported institutions of higher learning today.

The Execution of False Prophets (I Kings 18:40)

What shall we say of Elijah's treatment of the humiliated prophets of Baal? Should he not have reckoned their public disgrace sufficient punishment? Or should he not, perhaps, have enrolled them in the prophetic schools for indoctrination courses in the hope that they might gradually repent of their false religious concepts and turn to Jehovah? God, who knows the utter depths of human depravity (Jer. 13:23; 17:9), had already settled the question. False prophets were to die without mercy (Deut. 13:5; 18:20; cf. 7:2), for their words, like a deadly cancer, would spread confusion, unbelief, and ultimate disaster to all who heeded them (II Tim. 2:17).

---

[3]Refuted in *The New Bible Commentary: Revised* (Grand Rapids: Wm. B. Eerdmans Publishing Co., 1970), p. 344. For an excellent discussion of the entire Mt. Carmel episode, see Leon J. Wood, *Elijah, Prophet of God* (Des Plaines, Ill.: Regular Baptist Press, 1968), pp. 80-94.

Far more dangerous to the well-being of any people than thieves or even murderers are the disseminators of doctrinal error (Isa. 9:14-17; Matt. 23:15). If pollution of our natural resources and human bodies is becoming a national concern in America, what about the pollution of our minds and souls? Churches that emphasize social and political reform more than the Word of God are contributing to the ruin of the very nation they profess to love. The only churches that can expect Christ's commendation are those which examine and expose those who falsely claim to be Christ's representatives (Rev. 2:2). And so Elijah, rather than following his personal inclinations, obeyed God's Word (even as Samuel did when he "hewed Agag in pieces before Jehovah in Gilgal" — I Sam. 15:33), and led the nation in exterminating these promoters of theological error (see Zech. 13:3).

Elijah's Defeat (I Kings 18:41—19:6)

Baal, the supposed god of weather and fertility, had been totally discredited before the nation. Now Jehovah, the true Ruler of all nature, opened the windows of heaven "and there was a great rain." Perhaps in order to touch the king's heart and to convince him that he had no personal enmity against him, Elijah ran before Ahab's chariot along rain-soaked and muddy roads to the winter palace of Jezreel about fifteen miles to the east of Mt. Carmel.

But here the great prophet, physically and emotionally exhausted, made his greatest mistake. Instead of personally confronting Jezebel with what *Jehovah* had done, he allowed Ahab to tell Jezebel "all that *Elijah* had done." With astounding boldness, in her hardened depravity, Jezebel decided to intimidate Elijah with a threat on his life. (It is possible, however, that Jezebel feared his great power as a magician, for otherwise it seems that she would have killed him on the spot.) Unfortunately, the mere threat proved sufficient, for Elijah temporarily took his eyes from the Lord and, filled with fear, fled for his life.

Surprising though it may seem, this is one of the clearest evidences of the divine inspiration of this history. For if mere men had composed the account, they could hardly have resisted the temptation to omit or at least modify the record of their hero's spiritual failure. But this is the thing we need most to understand: apart from our blessed Saviour, no one, not even an apostle (cf. I Cor. 9:27; Gal. 2:11), is free from the disastrous potential of a sinful nature. Noah, Abraham, Moses, David, Solomon, and even John the Baptist, experienced failure and defeat because of sin. "Now these things happened unto them by way of example; and they were written for our admonition. . . . Wherefore let him that thinketh he standeth take heed lest he fall" (I Cor. 10:11, 12). Sinless perfection is a mere dream this side of heaven (I John 1:8-10), and God has been gracious to us in revealing that even Elijah "was a man of like passions with us" (James 5:17).

But the story of Elijah also proves this: "there hath no temptation taken you, but such as man can bear: but God is faithful, who will not suffer you to be tempted above that ye are able; but will with the temptation make also a way to escape, that ye may be able to endure it" (I Cor. 10:13). Elijah's failure is a deafening warning to the spiritually proud and complacent. But God's tender intervention on his behalf is a soothing reminder that "God is faithful" and that there is no need to despair. Like Jeremiah, who more than once wrote out his official resignation from the ministry (cf. Jer. 9:2; 20:7-18), Elijah prepared a formal speech for the Lord's record book: "It is enough; now, Jehovah, take away my life; for I am not better than my fathers" (I Kings 4).

This, of course, was no time for formal speeches and great decisions. The poor man was totally exhuasted (having travelled 150 miles from Jezreel to Beersheba, plus another day's journey, leaving his servant behind because he apparently had no intention of returning to his native land). Therefore the tender Shepherd of Israel (Isa. 40:11) simply ignored the speech, put His weary prophet to sleep, and commanded an angel to feed him when he woke up.

And so we too need to learn that things are never quite so bad for us as they may seem, for "we know that to them that love God all things work together for good" (Rom. 8:28). Elijah was not finished, because God was not finished. His greatest work was still in the future, even beyond the time of his departure from this world.[4] And that is true of each of us, too, if we love the Lord. For it is written, "Eye hath not seen, nor ear heard, neither have entered into the heart of man, the things which God hath prepared for them that love him. But God hath revealed them unto us by His Spirit" (I Cor. 2:9).

---

[4]See p. 66.

Chapter 5

ELIJAH: FROM MOUNT HOREB TO HEAVEN

Instruction at Horeb (I Kings 19:1-18)

Sometimes our service for God is hindered by neglect of the normal needs of the body for proper rest and nourishment: "It is vain for you to rise up early, to take rest late, to eat the bread of toil; for so he giveth unto his beloved sleep" (Ps. 127: 2). And so Elijah, after the terrific strain of his ministry on Mt. Carmel and his 150-mile marathon race from Jezreel to Beersheba and beyond, needed physical therapy at the hands of a tender angel. Rested, fed, and strengthened by the Lord, he journeyed 200 miles south from the vicinity of Beersheba across the trackless wilderness to the rugged mountain range of Horeb, to Mount Sinai, "the Mount of God" (cf. Exod. 3:1, 12; 4:27; 24:13). In fact, it may be that God led him to "*the* cave" (19:9, definite in Hebrew) where Moses was covered by God's "hand" lest he should see God's "face" (Exod. 33:22). Just as Moses desperately needed God's encouragement to lead the nation in a time of deep apostasy (Exod. 33:3-6, 15), so Elijah needed the same vision of God in his time of near despair.

God's instruction of the defeated prophet came in four phases. First, the deep probing of his heart: "What doest thou here, Elijah?" (compare God's question to Adam in Gen. 3:9). Elijah's answer revealed his keen disappointment and impatience with God's ways and an exaggerated pessimism concerning the condition of the nation. Why did not God strike Jezebel dead in his presence and then cause a great host of men to follow his spiritual leadership?

With the prophet's true attitude fully exposed, Jehovah now graciously showed him by a series of visual aids the drastic limitations of this method of dealing with men and nations. Great winds, earthquakes, and fires can quickly destroy men's lives (as God will demonstrate during the Great Tribulation — Rev. 6—18), but only by the "still small voice" of the Holy Spirit

60

can men be regenerated through the patient teaching of His Word (John 3:3-8; II Tim. 2:23-26).

Elijah's problem was shared by two of Jesus' own disciples, James and John, the sons of Zebedee. When a Samaritan village refused them hospitality because they were heading toward Jerusalem, James and John desired to consume them with fire from heaven — Elijah-style! But for this they were rebuked by the Saviour: "Ye know not what manner of spirit ye are of . . ." (Luke 9:55). And this in essense was God's rebuke to Elijah at Horeb.

This did not mean that judgment and destruction of sinful men had no part in God's program for Israel. God is not only gracious (I Kings 19:12; Exod. 34:6), but righteous (I Kings 19: 17; Exod. 34:7). Thus the third phase of his Horeb indoctrination course was that God *will* judge the wicked — in His own time and way! Hazael, Jehu, and Elisha were each to wield swords, though in very different ways, and Elijah would *directly* (in the case of Elisha) or *indirectly* (in the case of Hazael, II Kings 8:8-15; and Jehu, II Kings 9:1-10) launch them into their ministries of judgment.

The fourth point in God's instruction was this: in spite of outward appearances, God *is* doing a work in the hearts of men — "Yet will I leave me 7,000 in Israel . . . which have not bowed unto Baal" (19:18). So has it ever been from Adam to the present: "A remnant according to the election of grace" (Rom. 11:5). It may come as a shock to those who have little understanding of the height of God's holiness and the depth of man's depravity that the remnant of true believers is so small. This was Abraham's problem too, when he assumed that there were probably fifty righteous men in Sodom — or at the *very least,* ten (Gen. 18:22-33). Our Lord warned us that "few there be that find" eternal life (Matt. 7:14). But in the light of the frightening fact that apart from God's special grace *none* would be saved (Rom. 3:9-30), it should be a constant source of amazement that the Holy Spirit has transformed so many people (Rev. 7:9), and such unlikely people (I Cor. 1:27, 28), and under such unusual circumstances (cf. Phil. 4:22). Zealous to do our part in fulfilling God's great commission to the church, we must also be content with His gracious sovereignty in dealing with the nations.

Elisha Anointed (I Kings 19:15-21)

Perhaps Elijah never fully realized the significance for Israel of the anointing of Elisha. This great yet humble successor to the prophet of fire would have a ministry several times as long as Elijah's and one that would be filled with both miracle and blessing for many. We may assume that the two men had met before, even as Jesus had met Andrew, Peter, James and John several months before He called them to a life of ministry as fishers of men (cf. Matt. 4:19 with John 1:35-42).

Elisha was apparently a wealthy farmer, for he plowed with twelve yoke of oxen (he probably had eleven servants, each with one yoke); but when he heard God's call through Elijah, he forsook all and followed him. His desire to bid farewell to his parents was not a sign of hesitation on his part (contrast Jesus' rebuke of another potential disciple — Luke 9:61, 62). Instead, it was a desire to present a clear testimony to family and friends that God had called him to a great life work (compare Matthew's farewell testimony banquet — Luke 5:27-29).

Ahab Humiliated (I Kings 21:17-29)

It would be interesting to know what Ahab had been thinking about Elijah since he fled from the face of Jezebel. Had his magic powers left him, or had Jezebel plus her four hundred prophets of the Asherah proven too much for him? But he had not seen the last of God's prophet! As well might Ahab have sought to escape the presence of God in the uttermost part of the sea as to hide from the one whom God had specially prepared to activate the feeble conscience of Israel's monarch.

Having been goaded by Jezebel into the cold-blooded murder of Naboth and his sons (see pp. 44-45), Ahab stood at last in the beautiful vineyard he had so long coveted (cf. Isa. 5:8). Suddenly, like a nightmare become incarnate, Elijah appeared at the vineyard and pronounced judgment upon the guilty king. Even as Saul feared and even pursued Samuel because of his own guilty conscience (I Sam. 16:2; 19:22; 28:11), so now Ahab lashed out at his supposed tormentor: "Hast thou found me, O mine enemy?" (cf. I Kings 18:17). It has always been true, from the blood of righteous Abel to the death of the most recent Christian martyr, that the unsaved world seeks to alleviate the pressure of offended conscience by attacking those who speak God's Word (compare the fate of *Micaiah* in I Kings 22:27; *Hanani* in II Chron. 16:10; *Zechariah* in II Chron. 24:20-22; and *Jeremiah* in Jer. 26:8). It was a compliment to Elijah to be counted as an enemy of this royal murderer, for "friendship of the world is enmity with God" (James 4:4).

Elijah quickly explained that the king was really his *own* worst enemy! It was true that Jezebel had "stirred up" her husband to do things that had alienated the Lord and His prophet; and we may even go a step further and recognize that it was Satan who had stirred up Jezebel. But the *ultimate* fact, the fact that sealed his eternal doom, was that Ahab "did *sell himself* to do that which was evil in the sight of Jehovah" (I Kings 21:25). Two important points need to be made here. First, sin is a *personal* responsibility. Adam set the pattern for us all when he blamed Eve for his sin (Gen. 3:12; and Eve blamed Satan! — Gen. 3:13). But the partaking of the forbidden fruit was Adam's *own* fault, for the Scriptures make it perfectly clear that "by one man" sin entered into the world (Rom. 5:12) and that *"Adam was not beguiled"* (I Tim. 2:14). Secondly, sin is not freedom at all, but is the worst possible kind of *slavery* (Rom. 6:16; 7:14).

The blistering judgment had its appropriate effect upon Ahab. Recalling, perhaps, the fate of the 450 at Mt. Carmel, he humbled himself before Jehovah and "went softly." Weak rather than vicious in character (like Zedekiah the last king of Judah), Ahab's conscience was still functioning slightly. And because of this single response to his conscience, God extended his dynasty a dozen years! How vastly important in God's sight is our feeblest response to His Word! Only eternity will tell. How many months Ahab continued to go "softly" we cannot guess; but the following chapter (see comments, pp. 45-48) makes it clear that, like Pharaoh, he hardened his heart again.

Ahaziah Destroyed (I Kings 22:51-53; II Kings 1)

Though Ahaziah's name honored Jehovah ("Jehovah has grasped" — thus named by Ahab and Jezebel to please Jehoshaphat?), he made no concessions whatsoever to Israel's God. During his brief reign a joint ship-building enterprise with Jehoshaphat was destroyed by the Lord (II Chron. 20:37), and the Moabites ceased their vast tribute of wool to Israel (II Kings 1:1; 3:4). But his greatest claim to infamy was a futile military campaign against a one-man army named Elijah.

Seriously injured by a fall from the upper chamber of his palace, Ahaziah sent messengers to Philistia (about forty miles west) to inquire at a shrine of the god Baal-zebub at Ekron, thus showing himself to be a true son of Jezebel. The real name of this Syrian deity was Baal-zebul ("Lord of life"), but the Jews called him Baal-zebub ("Lord of the flies") in derision. By the time of Christ, this deity had become a symbol of Satan (Matt. 12:24).

However, the king's messengers were stopped en route by God's war machine, equipped with nothing but a garment of hair and a leather girdle. This dress was a forceful rebuke of the sinful luxury of the aristocracy of Israel, and became such a symbol of prophetic power that false prophets would "wear a hairy mantle to deceive" (Zech. 13:4)! Speaking of Elijah's later counterpart, John the Baptist, our Lord asked: "What went ye out to see? a man clothed in soft raiment?" (Matt. 11:8; cf. 3:4). But it was more than his rough garments and rugged visage that gave him power against Baal's henchmen — it was special authority from God Himself.

In the full fury of his wrath at this blatant challenge to his royal will, King Ahaziah flung one entire company of soldiers, and then another, against the impudent prophet, only to discover, to his horror, that the fire that fell at Mt. Carmel could consume people as well as bullocks! The third captain saw the light, surrendered to Elijah, and accompanied him to Samaria while the prophet personally (contrast I Kings 19:1) confronted the king with his appointed doom. Ahaziah's younger brother, Jehoram (Joram), far more diplomatic in his willingness to make outward concessions to Jehovah (II Kings 3:2, 10), but equally wicked in the sight of God (II Kings 3:13a), took the throne as the last of the Omri kings (cf. I Kings 21:29).

Heaven without Dying (II Kings 2:1-18)

Of Enoch's departure from this world it is simply recorded that he "walked with God: and was not; for God took him" (Gen. 5:24). Thus, "by faith Enoch was translated that he should not see death" (Heb. 11:5). Elijah was the only other man in history to share such an experience. In his hour of despair he had prayed: "O, Jehovah, take away my life" (I Kings 19:4). Not only was he not permitted to die then, but he never did die! This was God's way of honoring one who had sought so zealously to honor Him in a time of utter apostasy.

The prophet's march to heaven began at upper Gilgal (not the famous Gilgal of Joshua 4:20 near the bank of the Jordan) and moved steadily eastward and downward through Bethel and Jericho to the Jordan River. It was a testing time for young Elisha, for his master asked him three times to tarry behind (II Kings 2:2, 4, 6). Like Ruth the Moabitess, when encouraged by Naomi to avoid the uncertainties of a new adventure with the God of Israel, Elisha too may have replied: "entreat me not to leave thee, and to return from following after thee; for whither thou goest I will go. . . . Jehovah do so to me, and more also, if aught but death part thee and me" (Ruth 1:16, 17). For such courage and faithfulness, Elisha was promised a "double portion" of Elijah's spirit if he saw his master go up to heaven. The double portion was the portion of the firstborn son; namely twice as much as any other son (cf. Deut. 21:17). In other words, he would be Elijah's true successor in the prophetic ministry.

Refusing to be distracted by the unspiritual curiosity of the "sons of the prophets" (see discussion, p. 53) who had been told by the Lord a little of what might happen to him, and wielding his mantle like the rod of Moses, Elijah walked across the Jordan on dry ground. But this was nothing compared to what happened next. As the two men talked, they were suddenly parted from each other by a fiery chariot and horses from heaven (the chariot was the mightiest military instrument known to the ancient world and was therefore symbolic of God's incomparable power — Isa. 31:1; 66:15; Ps. 104:3, 4; Hab. 3:8, 9). While his faithful companion watched in wonder, Elijah was swept into the third heaven by a supernatural whirlwind leaving only his mantle for Elisha to cling to as the token of his new position and power.

Elijah left this earth in the year 852 B.C., and nearly nine hundred years later appeared again! Moses also appeared with him near the top of a high mountain in the presence of Jesus and three disciples. They talked with Jesus about His forthcoming death — a topic of never-ending fascination to dwellers in heaven (Luke 9:27-36; cf. I Peter 1:12; Rev. 5:9, 12). But the purpose of this appearance was to glorify Jesus, not Moses and Elijah. For when Peter foolishly ("knowing not what he said") suggested the erection of *three* tabernacles, thus putting Moses and Elijah on a par with Jesus, a cloud immediately overshadowed the two prophets, "and lifting up their eyes, they saw no one, save Jesus only" (Matt. 17:8). Great though they were in the history of Israel, Moses and Elijah were mere men, and sinful ones at that.[1]

---

[1]See Alva J. McClain, *The Greatness of The Kingdom* (Chicago: Moody Press, 1968), pp. 181, 337, 457, for helpful discussions of Elijah's future ministry to Israel.

Chapter 6

ELISHA: FROM THE JORDAN TO SHUNEM

A New Beginning (II Kings 2:13-18)

Like Joshua, the tried and proven successor to Moses, who crossed the Jordan by the miraculous power of God, Elisha exercised his new prophetic authority by wielding the mantle of his master, and "the Jordan was driven back" (Ps. 114:3b). Even if the nation rejected him, at least the forces of nature seemed fully aware of the "double portion" of Elijah's spirit that was now his, and this must have been most encouraging to the young prophet. If the enemies of God thought that His power was crippled by the disappearance of Elijah, they would soon discover otherwise!

On the west bank of the Jordan, Elisha was greeted by fifty sons of the prophets (II Kings 2:15). They had known that Elijah would be taken by the Lord (II Kings 2:5), but they refused to believe Elisha's story about his master's bodily ascension. Refusing to argue with such immature minds concerning an experience so spiritually precious (just as our Lord never publicly proclaimed His virgin birth, and Paul waited fourteen years before sharing his experience in the third heaven — II Cor. 12: 1-4), he sent the stubborn students on a futile three-day expedition to recover the broken body of Elijah from the trans-Jordan mountains.

Bethel and the Bears (II Kings 2:23-25)

Leaving the region of Jericho (see p. 72 for a discussion of the miracle of healed waters), Elisha climbed fifteen miles to the city of Bethel, retracing his steps with Elijah. But before he could visit the school of the prophets there (II Kings 2:3), he was challenged by a large mob of irresponsible young delinquents. The expression "young lads" (II Kings 2:23) certainly

67

does not mean little children.[1] The same terms are used of David when Samuel anointed him (I Sam. 16:11), and by then David had already established a reputation as "a mighty man of valor" (I Sam. 16:18), having killed a lion and a bear (I Sam. 17:34-37). So these were young unmarried men, perhaps from twelve to thirty years of age, idle and "vile fellows of the rabble" (Acts 17:5) who were available for hire to perpetrate almost any act of violence. And in the light of their words to Elisha, and his response, it seems highly probable that the calf-worshipping priests of Bethel had master-minded this plot, in order to discredit and humiliate Elijah's successor.

The taunt, "Go up . . . go up" may have been intended as a mockery of the supposed ascension of Elijah. If even the sons of the prophets at Jericho refused to believe Elisha's story of this stupendous miracle, what could be expected from the unbelievers in Israel? And the expression "thou baldhead" was one of extreme contempt. They were pronouncing a divine curse upon him, for which baldness was often the outward sign (cf. Isa. 3: 17a, 24).

Since this was an *official* challenge to his God-appointed ministry, Elisha "cursed them in the name of Jehovah," and in remarkable fulfillment of Moses' warning against national apostasy, two wild animals leaped upon the mob and forty-two were wounded ("if ye walk contrary unto me . . . I will send the beast of the field among you, which shall rob you of your children . . ." — Lev. 26:21, 22). This was a shocking, but comparatively mild warning to the nation of what would soon follow if the general apostasy continued. However, instead of repenting of their sins and turning to God, "they mocked the messengers of God, and despised his words, and *scoffed at his prophets,* until the wrath of Jehovah arose against his people, till there was no remedy" (II Chron. 36:16). No wild animals could match the savage cruelty that would be heaped upon this hard-

---

[1]Critics of the O.T. concept of Jehovah love to emphasize the youth and innocence of these lads. Thus, H. W. F. Saggs states that the O.T. "records, with obvious satisfaction, the fate of forty-two cheeky urchins, cursed by Elisha and in consequence eaten by bears" (*The Greatness That Was Babylon,* New York, Mentor Books, 1968), p. 240.

ened people by that specially-prepared rod of God's anger, the Assyrian army; and that rod would strike within four generations.[2]

The Moabite Campaign (II Kings 3)

When King Ahab died, the Moabites rebelled against Israel. Ahaziah was unable to cope with this crisis, so it was left to his brother, Jehoram. In the providence of God, a most remarkable inscription was discovered in 1868 (see Fig. 8) which contains the actual words of Mesha, king of Moab: "As for Omri, king of Israel, he humbled Moab many years, for Chemosh was angry at his land. And his son [Ahab] followed him and he also said, 'I will humble Moab.' In my time he spoke thus, but I have triumphed over him and over his house, while Israel hath perished for ever!"[3]

Determined to recover his lost source of tribute, Jehoram recruited the services of the ever-willing Jehoshaphat (cf. I Kings 22:4; II Chron. 20:35-37), the father-in-law of his sister Athaliah. In addition, he enlisted the King of Edom, who had reasons of his own to seek revenge upon Moab (cf. II Chron. 20:23, where "Mt. Seir" refers to Edom).

As the combined armies moved across the barren wilderness south of the Dead Sea, no fresh water could be found, and their plight became desperate. King Jehoram blamed Jehovah for this; but Jehoshaphat, remembering that God had spared his life because of his desire to hear a true prophet (I Kings 22), once again asked for a prophet of Jehovah. When a servant suggested Elisha, he recognized his name; but it is surprising that his presence in the expedition was not known before this. Possibly he intended to serve in the capacity of a modern chaplain, providing systematic instruction for the few officers and men who would be willing to hear God's Word.

God greatly honored the young prophet by bringing these three kings to his feet! Later, the King of Syria would do the same (II Kings 8:9) — a true foretaste of the day when "all

[2]See Richard Messner, "Elisha and the Bears," *Grace Journal* (Spring, 1962).

[3]Pritchard, *ANET,* p. 320.

8. The Moabite Stone. This inscription records Israel's conquest of Moab and the successful revolt of Mesha, king of Moab. Courtesy, Oriental Institute.

kings shall fall down before him [the Messiah], and all nations
shall serve him" (Ps. 72:11; cf. Isa. 49:23). But Elisha, unim-
pressed by the array of royalty, denounced Jehoram to his face:
"What have I to do with thee? get thee to the prophets of thy
father, and to the prophets of thy mother" (II Kings 3:13). In
other words, Baal's worshippers should consult Baal's prophets.
The privilege of answered prayer is granted by God only to
those who ask "according to his will" (I John 5:14). But for the
sake of Jehoshaphat, whose outward compromises disguised a
heart that loved the Lord, Elisha agreed to consult Jehovah.

At first glance, it would seem strange that Elisha would ask
for a minstrel to play for him. This was not to awaken any
latent magical powers of the prophet, as Jehoram probably assumed, but was rather for the purpose of calming his distraught
soul in order that he might concentrate upon God Himself.
Similarly (though the situation was quite different) when David
played on his harp, "Saul was refreshed, and was well, and the
evil spirit departed from him" (I Sam. 16:23; cf. I Chron. 25:1).
Music is one of God's greatest means for thrilling man's heart
with His glory and grace (Ps. 150:3-6; Eph. 5:19; Rev. 5:8, 9),
and Elisha was fully aware of this fact. God heard the fervent
prayer of His prophet and not only filled the region with water
but also delivered the enemy into their hands.

Seeing his hopes for victory deteriorating, the desperate king
of Moab offered his eldest son as a sacrifice to the god Chemosh
on the top of the city wall. This was the supreme act of devotion to a pagan deity, and Jehovah had long since warned Israel
against such abominations (Deut. 12:31; Micah 6:7).[4] The superstitious (and increasingly polytheistic) Israelites were so terrified at the prospect of what Chemosh, the god of Moab, would
do in response to this supreme sacrifice, that they gave up the
siege and returned to their own land![5] And so it was, as in the
days of Elisha's predecessor, that the nation continued to halt
between two opinions as to who their God really was.

---

[4]For an explanation of God's command to Abraham to sacrifice Isaac,
see David Dilling, "The Atonement and Human Sacrifice," *Grace Journal*
(Winter 1964).

[5]See George Harton, "The Meaning of II Kings 3:27," *Grace Journal*
(Fall, 1970).

Water, Oil, Pottage, Loaves and Axe-heads
(II Kings 2:19-22; 4:1-7, 38-44; 6:1-7)

One of the truly outstanding truths about our God is that He concerns Himself with apparently insignificant people and their little problems. He is so great that He must humble Himself just to look into the universe He created (Ps. 113:6)! But the same transcendent God "raiseth up the poor out of the dust and . . . maketh the barren woman to keep house, and to be a joyful mother of children" (Ps. 113:7-9)! While maintaining the orbits of stars and planets, He also numbers the very hairs of our heads (Matt. 10:30). This must be so, if He is truly God, for even human minds realize that *total control* of a system must include the control of all the minute parts and events that make up that system. That seems to be the message of these portions of Scripture.

The miracles of Elijah's brief ministry were mainly spectacular in character, involving the entire nation. But even then, it was not beneath the dignity of Elijah (and Elijah's God) to care for the needs of a widow in Zarephath by miraculous intervention (I Kings 17:13-24). Elisha's ministry, on the other hand, involved numerous "small" miracles by which the temporal needs of God's servants were graciously met.

First was the healing of Jericho's waters (II Kings 2:19-22), a miracle of blessing that stands in sharp contrast to the miracle of cursing which followed (see pp. 67-69). Even as God commanded Moses to use a tree as a symbol of His power to purify the brackish waters at Marah (Exod. 15:25), so Elisha used salt. Obviously, neither the tree nor the salt had any intrinsic powers. To this very day, tourists are shown "Elisha's pool" near the town of Jericho — if nothing else, at least a token of the deep impression this miracle has made upon the minds of men.

Second was the miracle of the widow's oil (II Kings 4:1-7). A poor seminary student died, leaving nothing but unpaid debts for his widow. To make matters worse, her two sons were about to be taken by the creditor to work for him until the debt was paid. This may seem cruel to us, but it is important to note that the creditor is not depicted as a villain in this episode. Bond-service for debt payment was part of God's plan for Israel, but

He also safeguarded this system from abuses (Lev. 25:39-55; Matt. 18:25). Instead of denouncing the creditor, Elisha commanded the widow to pay her full debt (II Kings 4:7). God commands His people to honor their rightful obligations (cf. Rom. 13:8), even under inconvenient circumstances.

The increasing of the widow's oil supply was proportionate to her faith and obedience in borrowing the empty vessels. It must have been somewhat embarrassing to explain to her neighbors why she needed all of these; but even though the miracle took place behind closed doors, the whole neighborhood must have rejoiced in the results when they saw their oil-filled pots being sold and payment made to the creditor instead of the widow surrendering her two sons to the creditor. When the veil has been removed, we will find that God has not only supplied all our needs, but has done so in the most glorious possible way (Phil. 4:19).

The third and fourth "minor miracles" in Elisha's ministry (II Kings 4:38-44) involved food supplies for hungry seminary students at Upper Gilgal (cf. II Kings 2:1). One student, possibly meditating on Elisha's fascinating theology lectures, carelessly gathered some poisonous wild cucumbers to add to the luncheon stew. God graciously overruled this potential tragedy for good and demonstrated once again that He "will add all these things unto us" if we seek His interests first.

Soon afterwards a believer from a nearby town brought the first recorded "seminary offering" — an inadequate supply in the form of barley loaves and grain. Gehazi revealed his typical lack of faith (cf. II Kings 4:27; 6:15), but God chose to multiply the offering and thus to anticipate the far greater miracle of our Lord beside the Sea of Galilee. Little things become great when they are dedicated to God.

Last, and perhaps most fascinating of all, was the miracle of the floating axe-head (II Kings 6:1-7). Could anything have been less important in the history of Israel than the loss of an iron axe-head in the Jordan by a careless student? Perhaps not, in man's estimation; but the event must be seen in proper context to be appreciated. The theological students at Jericho suffered in their studies from inadequate housing facilities. The great prophet of God was asked to join with them in their little venture of faith, the construction of a dormitory. Inexperienced and poorly equipped (their tools were borrowed), they nevertheless worked with zeal and for the glory of God. Is the great God of the universe interested in such projects? We might laugh at their feeble effort, but God's question is this: "Who hath despised the day of small things?" (Zech. 4:10). When the horrified student saw the borrowed tool sink deep into the river, both he and his companions gained a never-to-be-forgotten insight into God's loving concern for His own when He put forth His hand and "made the iron to swim." Later, the Lord Jesus taught a frustrated disciple a similar lesson when He commanded a fish to pick up a coin from the depth of the sea and bring it to the shore (Matt. 17:27). God, not man, determines which events are the most important.

The Shunammite's Son (II Kings 4:8-37)

On the northern edge of the Plain of Esdraelon, north of Jezreel and east of Mt. Carmel, was a little town named Shunem. Like Bethany near Jerusalem, it will always be remembered as the place where one returned from the realm of death to mortal life.

The background to the miracle may not be spectacular, but it is full of interest. A wealthy lady of Shunem provided a "prophet's chamber" in her home for Elisha's convenience during his frequent travels in that region. Desiring to show her a special favor in response to her gracious hospitality, Elisha offered to speak for her to the king or to the captain of the host if she had any complaint against a neighbor or government official. The prophet apparently had access to the royal court at this time because of the victory over Moab which he was instrumental in achieving (Chap. 3). But she lived in peace with her neighbors and needed no special intercession (I Kings 4:13).

This was the setting for two of the greatest miracles of the Old Testament. First, God granted to her a son when her husband was old (like the fathers of Isaac and John the Baptist). Second, when this miracle boy (whose name is not even recorded!) died, he was brought back to life again. The Scriptures make is very plain that the Shunammite's son did not merely fall into a coma (cf. II Kings 4:20, 32; 8:5). It is also quite clear that no mere sacred object (Elisha's staff) or ceremony (laying it on the child's face) could bring life.

Somehow, the Shunammite woman knew that Gehazi lacked the depth of faith that Elisha possessed. And so, hurrying to Mt. Carmel (ten miles to the west) where she and others had received from Elisha systematic instruction in God's Word in times past, she insisted on seeing the prophet himself in her hour of deepest need (II Kings 4:24, 27, 30). Gehazi, whose spiritual shallowness was later fully exposed (II Kings 5), was completely helpless in the presence of death, even with Elisha's equipment and methods at his disposal. This is an exceedingly important point. God is a glorious Person, and cannot be manipulated by sinful man under any circumstances.

Doubtless remembering Elijah's explanation to him of how God had raised the widow's son at Zarephath (I Kings 17), Elisha demanded privacy and time for fervent prayer. Elijah had stretched himself three times upon the dead child before God granted life. But Elisha did this only twice, and after the first time he could detect warmth returning to the boy's flesh. Why God directed Elijah and Elisha to employ such methods we cannot know; but it is emphatically clear that God, not the methods, brought life. But great as these miracles were, we cannot help but contrast them with the simplicity and majesty of our Lord's work of raising the dead: a mere word (Lazarus and the widow of Nain's son) or touch of the hand (Jairus' daughter).

Elisha then warned the Shunammite to take her family to Philistia to escape a seven-year judgment-drought upon the land, which probably coincided with the final years of King Jehoram (II Kings 8:1). When she returned, she found that her property had been confiscated, but she also found that the Omri-Ahab dynasty had been destroyed (in the persons of Queen Jezebel and her son Jehoram), and that Jehu was now on the throne. Gehazi was telling Jehu about Elisha's miracles, especially the raising of the Shunammite's son. Just then, they were brought into the king's presence and received his assistance in regaining her property. Thus did Jehovah honor His prophet, even in high places.

Chapter 7

ELISHA: MIRACLES IN LIFE AND IN DEATH

Naaman the Syrian (II Kings 5)

The miraculous healing of Naaman the Syrian actually occurred *later* than the events of Chapters 6, 7, and the first part of Chapter 8; because in these chapters Gehazi, Elisha's servant, is seen in positions of honor (cf. II Kings 6:17; 8:4). This would be unthinkable if he had already experienced the permanent curse of leprosy (II Kings 5:27). Thus, the cursing of Gehazi must have occurred soon after his visit with the king (II Kings 8:1-6).

Apparently lepers were not ostracized from society in Syria; or else Naaman had proved himself so indispensable to the king (probably Hazael at this time) that his leprosy was tolerated. In the marvellous providence of God, a servant girl from Israel attended his wife and boasted of Elisha's great power to help people, even to raising the dead (II Kings 4:35). If only Christians today would speak this enthusiastically about the powers of their great Saviour!

When the King of Syria heard about the Israelite prophet, he immediately prepared an enormous gift for the King of Israel (more than $80,000 in value), assuming that the King would then bribe his court prophet to perform his magical powers on behalf of this foreign dignitary. But the King of Israel (possibly Jehoahaz by this time, because Jehu would have known about the powers of Elisha — II Kings 8:4) not only ignored Elisha but took the request as a subtle means of exposing his human frailty as a royal representative of Jehovah.

Elisha was deeply offended by this willful ignoring of his position as God's prophet, even as Elijah had challenged King Ahaziah for sending to a foreign god for help (II Kings 1:3). It is encouraging at least that the king must have acknowledged his error, and sent Naaman, in all his military splendor, to the door of Elisha's humble abode (cf. II Kings 3:12; 8:8). A greater contrast can hardly be imagined!

To put this mighty one into the right position before Jehovah, Elisha refused to see him personally, and instructed him to wash seven times in the muddy Jordan. No magic incantation or mysterious handwaving (nor all the clean waters of the rivers of Damascus) could solve this man's problem — only the direct intervention of the living God. Would he be willing to do a very simple and apparently foolish thing, believing that God could meet his need according to His promise? That is the essence of the gospel as it goes forth to men today. The vast majority of men consider the crucified Jesus to be an utterly foolish way to deal with the leprosy of sin (I Cor. 1:23); but to those who have taken God at His word, such a message has become the very power and wisdom of God (I Cor. 1:24; Rom. 1:16).

Naaman must have felt rather silly coming up the sixth time with nothing to show for it; but the seventh time, like the final encirclement of Jericho (Josh. 6:16, 20), was the moment of miracle. With skin as fresh and clean as a little child's (cf. Matt. 18:3), the deeply grateful foreigner returned to offer thanks (like the Samaritan leper of Luke 17:15) and to give him a gift. Much in the way of testimony and principle was at stake here. If Elisha accepted the money, Naaman would have been confirmed in his view that even Jehovah's miracles are for hire, just as Simon Magus thought he could buy the power to bestow the gifts of the Spirit (Acts 8:18-20).

Another superstitious view Naaman had was that no god could be properly worshipped except in his own land. Therefore, he would take some of Jehovah's land back to Damascus with him! Also, while accompanying his master in public worship in the heathen temple, he would pray to Jehovah while bowing to Rimmon (or Hadad), the god of Damascus. It will be remembered that the Apostle Paul was willing to make large concessions to weak believers on non-essential matters (Acts 18:18; 21:26; I Cor. 8:13; 9:22; 10:28); and in spite of the problems inherent in this passage, we must assume that Elisha considered Naaman to be ill-prepared for advanced instruction in the worship of Jehovah at this moment. Thus the concession: "Go in peace" (II Kings 5:19).

Now comes a shattering blow to this otherwise refreshing scene: "But Gehazi . . ."! Our hearts are deeply wounded, as was Elisha's (II Kings 5:26) at the shocking betrayal by Gehazi, and even more by the spoiled vision of God's free grace that Naaman doubtless carried with him to the grave. The plot was well executed. The money and the raiment were not to be for himself, but for two poor students preparing for the ministry. Naaman doubled the amount of money requested, glad at last for the opportunity to pay for his healing (cf. II Kings 5:15, 16), and even sent two servants to carry the garments and the 150 pounds of precious metal all the way to Gehazi's house.

Should not Elisha's servant have guessed that God would see him? How blinding sin can be! Elisha clarified Gehazi's vision (compare the earlier experience recorded in II Kings 6:17): with multitudes of people in desperate spiritual need and false prophets abounding, was this a time for God's servants to seek wealth (to say nothing of seeking it by dishonest means)? In proportion to his privileges, so also was his judgment — perpetual, inheritable leprosy! And thus, for one more of God's privileged servants came the judgment that Paul feared so much: "lest by any means, after that I have preached to others, I myself should be rejected" (I Cor. 9:27).

Elisha and the Syrian Army (II Kings 6:8-23)

Long before the healing of Naaman, while Benhadad I was still king of Syria (II Kings 6:24), a most remarkable thing happened: an entire Syrian army was captured alive by Elisha the prophet! It all began with a series of raiding expeditions against the eastern borders of Israel. When these were all systematically and mysteriously blocked, a servant of Benhadad suggested that Elisha was responsible (II Kings 6:12). Whereupon, the king sent an entire army, complete with chariots, to capture him! Possibly he hoped to bribe the prophet into becoming *his* court magician!

By night the army surrounded the city of Dothan, and early the next morning Gehazi looked in utter terror at the scene around him: "Alas, my master! how shall we do?" Elisha's calm reply provides one of the greatest assurances the believer can have: "They that are with us are greater than they that are with them" (cf. II Chron. 32:7; I John 4:4). Then Gehazi's eyes were opened, and things took on a new perspective: it is not God's people, but God's enemies who are surrounded and helpless (cf. II Kings 19:28)! When overwhelmed by the forces of evil, we too need to look up and see, with the eye of faith, the heavenly hosts that serve God night and day; for it is always true that "the angel of Jehovah encampeth round about them that fear him, and delivereth them" (Ps. 34:7).

The blindness which God inflicted upon the Syrians did not permanently damage their eyes, but was an intensive form of mental blindness. The only other occurrence of this Hebrew word (sanwērîm) describes the judgment of the Sodomites who attacked Lot's home (Gen. 19:11). Mocking the frustrated Syrians (as Elijah had mocked the Baal prophets on Mt. Carmel), he led them to the capital city (cf. II Kings 5:3) ten miles away, in what must have been one of the strangest looking processions in history!

The king of Israel (probably the wicked Jehoram) saw this as an opportunity for an easy and cruel triumph over his hated enemy; but God could not honor a faithless ruler with such a victory. Furthermore, this would be one more opportunity to confirm in the thinking of the Syrians that "the kings of the house of Israel are merciful kings" (I Kings 20:31), because their God is a merciful God. The Syrians must have been greatly impressed, not only with Jehovah's mercy, but also with Elisha's superhuman insight, "for the bands of Syria came no more into the land of Israel" (II Kings 6:23).

The Siege of Samaria (II Kings 6:24—7:20)

After the lessons of the previous futile invasion had worn off, Ben-hadad determined to destroy Samaria once and for all (II Kings 6:24). As the siege continued, the plight of the surrounded Israelites became desperate. Even an ass's head (not ordinarily a choice item!) brought 80 shekels of silver; and four pints of dove's dung was worth five shekels of silver (for fuel). Just as God had warned through Moses long before, willful national rebellion against His Word would reduce His proud and privileged people to savage cannibalism (Lev. 26:29; Deut. 28:

53; cf. Lam. 4:10), as He gave them up to the outworking of their own carnal desires.

Just like his mother Jezebel, King Jehoram placed all the blame for this crisis upon God's prophet (II Kings 6:31; cf. I Kings 19:2). Probably Elisha had warned the king before the siege began that such a judgment would come if the nation did not repent. Jehoram now felt that a quick way to end the siege would be to kill Elisha and thus break his evil spell upon the city (II Kings 6:33). By such thoughts he demonstrated that he was indeed a "son of a murderer" (a Hebrew idiom for murderer, or possibly a reference to his father Ahab who had murdered Naboth). An executioner was immediately sent to behead the prophet, but he was transfixed by the words he heard even as the Temple guards returned empty-handed from their commission to capture Jesus with the strangest of excuses: "Never man so spake" (John 7:32, 46).

Within twenty-four hours, said Elisha, the famine would not only be ended, but a whole measure of fine flour would sell for a shekel! (Recall that during the siege *eighty* shekels would buy only an ass's head.) And this fantastic deflation of prices would be accomplished by courtesy of the Syrian army, which would leave their rich supplies behind while fleeing from an army that did not exist. Four humble and desperate men, ostracized from the community because of their leprosy, were honored by God with the great discovery (cf. Ps. 113:7, 8); and fearing divine punishment if they failed to share the good news with their starving countrymen, they hurried back to Samaria to inform the porter at the city gate. The analogy to our own situation is obvious. God has utterly routed our great enemy through the work of His Son. But if we, who have made the great discovery, fail to share it with those who are dying in their sins, we will be held accountable to God (II Cor. 5:11-20). The responsibility we bear is far greater than that of the four lepers of Samaria.

When the report of the lepers was confirmed, the half-starved survivors poured out of the city gates and gorged themselves on the fine flour and barley they found strewn all over the fields (causing the black market in asses' heads and dove's dung to collapse immediately!). The captain of the guard who had been appointed by the king to supervise an orderly exodus through the city gate not only became a victim of the stampede but a literal fulfillment of Elisha's enigmatic and somber prophecy: "Behold, thou shalt see it with thine eyes, but shalt not eat thereof" (II Kings 7:17-20). We may be sure, however, that in the midst of all the rush and confusion few, if any, took the trouble to thank Elisha or Elisha's God for this miraculous intervention on their behalf (cf. Ps. 78:29-32; 106:15).

Elisha in Damascus (II Kings 8:7-15)

About ten years had passed since Elijah's ascension, and his successor now carried out a special commission God had entrusted to him — the anointing of Hazael to be king of Syria (cf. I Kings 19:15). The aged and sick king, Ben-hadad I, granted to Elisha a royal reception in Damascus. Sending his captain, Hazael, to meet him with a caravan of forty camels' burden of Damascene delicacies for a gift (somewhat inappropriate for the rugged prophet!), he hoped to purchase the prophet's magical healing powers for his own physical needs. Elisha's reputation was very high in Syria at this time, probably because of his single-handed conquest of the Syrian army at Dothan, and his merciful treatment of the captives (II Kings 6:23).

What did Elisha mean by his statement to Hazael: "Go, say unto him, Thou shalt surely recover; howbeit Jehovah hath showed me that he shall surely die"? At first sight, the statement seems to be completely contradictory. Why tell the king he would recover if God had revealed to the prophet that he would die? There are two ways to interpret these words. The first is that Elisha, knowing that wicked Hazael would not tell his master the truth concerning his imminent death, commanded him to carry out his lying scheme; just as God told Balaam to go with the messengers of Balak (Num. 22:20-22), and as Jesus told Judas to begin his diabolical work of betrayal (John 13:27). The second possibility is that it would not be the illness, but the murderous Hazael who would end the king's life. In either case, it is perfectly clear from the context (in spite of II Kings 8:13b) that Elisha did not put any wicked thoughts into Hazael's mind — they were already there!

As the Lord began to show the prophet what would happen to thousands of Israelites at the hands of this cruel man, he stared at him in fascination, and then broke down and wept. And as we look back upon the fulfillment (II Kings 10:32; 13: 3-7, 22; in the light of Amos 1:3-5), we may weep too.

Telling Ben-hadad only half of the prophet's words (II Kings 8:14), which in this situation was equivalent to uttering a complete lie, Hazael dipped a bedspread into water and smothered him to death. We are not told whether Elisha actually anointed Hazael or not (cf. I Kings 19:15), but his cold-blooded murder of Ben-hadad demonstrated that a new scourge in the hand of God was now ready (in spite of Hazael's mock humility — II Kings 8:13) for the chastening of His stubborn people.[1]

The Death of Elisha (II Kings 13:14-21)

Elijah's prophetic ministry lasted less than a decade; but his great successor continued a ministry of miracle and teaching throughout the reigns of Jehoram, Jehu, Jehoahaz, and Joash (or Jehoash) — a total of at least fifty-five years! At last, the aged prophet found himself upon his death-bed (II Kings 13:14). The year was now about 795 B.C., and the King of Israel, Joash, came down to visit him.

The natural sadness of the scene was magnified by the king's reminder that Elijah had not died, but was raptured to heaven. Would not God do the same for Elisha — one who had served Him so long and so faithfully? But our Lord is not obliged to do for one of His servants what He does for another, and we may be sure that Elisha was well aware of this fact. If he had ever asked the Lord for a repetition of Elijah's whirlwind rapture, we can almost hear His reply: "If I willed that he should thus depart from the earth, what is that to thee? follow thou me" (cf. John 21:21-23).

It is just possible, however, that Joash's quotation of Elisha's cry, "My father, my father, the chariots of Israel and the horsemen thereof" was his way of saying: "I want to be *your* successor and to inherit the portion of the firstborn that you received from

---

[1]See p. 84 for Elisha's part in the anointing of Jehu.

Elijah." If so, then the symbolic military campaign which Elisha told him to wage against Syria with bow and arrows was the test to determine his fitness for such a privileged position.

In any case, the king's half-hearted response to Elisha's command brought deep disappointment to the prophet. For forty years Hazael had attacked the Holy Land with unique cruelty and persistence; and now his son Ben-hadad II was on the throne to perpetuate his dreadful work (II Kings 13:3). Would King Joash be willing to trust Jehovah for full victory against the enemy? Apparently noi, and for the same reason that Ahab had spared the life of Ben-hadad I many years before (I Kings 20:34), namely, the worldly desire for military security through maintaining Syria as a buffer state against the even more frightful threat of Assyria.

We must assume that Joash understood perfectly the symbolism of the acts Elisha commanded him to perform (compare the iron horns in I Kings 22:11). Five or six strikes upon the ground with a handful of arrows meant total victory over Syria. Four or less would mean partial victory. Joash deliberately rejected God's way and chose his own. Therefore, so far from being a successor to Elisha's prophetic office, Joash was not even qualified to fulfill his own kingly office, and God gave him only limited victory against the enemy (II Kings 13:25).

Elisha's Posthumous Ministry (II Kings 13:20, 21)

Elisha was not taken to heaven in a whirlwind; but God granted him an experience recorded of no other in history. After he died and was buried, the body of an Israelite soldier killed while defending the land from Moabite invaders was hastily dropped into Elisha's sepulchre. As his body touched the bones of Elisha, his life was restored to him and he stood on his feet! If it could be said of Abel that "he being dead yet speaketh" (Heb. 11:4), we might say of Elisha that he, being dead, yet ministered! And if the other one whom Elisha raised from the dead (the Shunammite's son, now nearing sixty years of age) could have met this soldier, they would have agreed that even without a whirlwind ascension, Elisha was surely one of the greatest servants God ever had.

Chapter 8

FROM JEHU TO THE ASSYRIAN CAPTIVITY

Jehu Anointed King of Israel (II Kings 9:1-13)

Elisha had personally fulfilled the commission God had given to Elijah to anoint Hazael king of Syria (I Kings 19:15; II Kings 8:8-15); but he delegated to one of the "sons of the prophets" the task of finding and anointing Jehu to be king of Israel. Perhaps Elisha wanted to avoid giving the impression that he was personally responsible for or in favor of the policies of Jehu.

The rush and confusion of Jehu's anointing seemed to be prophetic of the entire career of this mad militarist. As Jehu and his captains were seated in a council of war in Ramoth-gilead near the battlefront, a wild-eyed young prophet burst upon the scene, invited Jehu into a nearby house, anointed him as king of Israel with the primary commission of annihilating the dynasty of Omri and Ahab, and then fled away. When the captains found out what had happened, they immediately improvised a throne, placed their garments beneath him as an act of homage (as many did for the Lord Jesus at His triumphal entry into Jerusalem), blew the trumpet and shouted, "Jehu is king" (compare Absalom, II Sam. 15:10; and Solomon, I Kings 1:39).

Jehoram and Jezebel Slain (II Kings 9:14-37)

Determined to get back to Jezreel before Jehoram could hear of the coronation and organize his forces, Jehu drove "furiously" (same root as the word used for the "mad" prophet, II Kings 9:11) in his chariot with a company of soldiers. The wounded Jehoram, anxious to hear news of the battle, sent messengers to enquire, "Is all well?" (II Kings 9:17, ASV margin). Increasingly suspicious of foul play, Jehoram took Ahaziah (his sister's son, now king of Judah), and dashed forth, in spite of his infirmities, to confront Jehu face to face. Like a mighty magnet, Naboth's blood drew the kings to the fateful spot where Elijah had pronounced doom upon Ahab and his dynasty (I Kings 21:21-22). Unrepentant to the last, and with the judgment of God ringing in his ears, Jehoram king of Israel died like his father, and his nephew suffered a like fate soon afterward.

Jezebel knew what was coming. If she had to die, she would do so like a Phoenician queen, with painted eyes, set hair, and with defiance spewing from her mouth: "Is it peace, thou Zimri, thy master's murderer?" (II Kings 9:31). Zimri had boldly destroyed Baasha's dynasty, but paid the penalty by dying in flames a week later (I Kings 16:9-20) while under attack from Omri, Ahab's father. The palace eunuchs were doubtless glad to demonstrate their loyalty to the new king by throwing Jezebel to her death. Once again God's word was fulfilled to the letter as her body was devoured by scavenger dogs because of Jehu's unintentional (?) delay in granting her the burial of "a king's daughter."

Jehu, the Scourge of God (II Kings 10:1-36)

Intoxicated by his spectacular victory over Ahab's widow, son, and grandson, Jehu now challenged the rulers and elders of Samaria to a formal combat to determine the destiny of the kingdom. By his various wives and concubines (cf. I Kings 20:3-5 and II Kings 10:1 for hints of the size of Ahab's harem) Ahab had left seventy sons in Samaria who were cared for by foster-fathers (compare the seventy sons of Gideon — Judges 8:30). But it was perfectly obvious that not one of them had the character or experience to lead the nation in a struggle against Jehu. So the nobles accepted the drastic terms of surrender and brought to Jezreel seventy baskets containing the heads of Ahab's sons. Mimicking the terror-tactics of the king of Assyria (to whom he would bow in abject submission before the year was over),[1] Jehu demanded that the heads be placed in two heaps at the entrance of the city gate so that all who passed through would have second thoughts about any possible revolt. Shalmaneser III thus describes his method of handling conquered cities: "I slew with the sword 300 of their warriors. Pillars of skulls I erected in front

---

[1]The Black Obelisk of Shalmaneser III, dated 841 B.C. (Jehu's first year), shows Jehu bowing to the king (see Fig. 9). The caption begins: "The tribute of Jehu, son of Omri; I received from him silver, gold. . ." (ANET, p. 281).

9. The Black Obelisk of Shalmaneser III. In the second panel may be seen "Jehu, son of Omri" kneeling before the Assyrian king. The cuneiform text describes the tribute received by Shalmaneser. Courtesy, Oriental Institute.

of the town. . . . In the moat of the town I piled them up, I covered the wide plain with the corpses of their fighting men, I dyed the mountains with their blood like red wool. I erected pillars of skulls in front of his town."[2]

Jehu then sought to gain the favor of the populace by pointing out that he had not personally executed Ahab's sons. Nevertheless, their death was clear evidence that God meant exactly what He had said through Elijah the prophet (which Jehu had heard with his own ears — II Kings 9:25). This does not necessarily mean that Jehu was a disciple of Elijah or of Elijah's God, for he could favor a Jehovah-religion as opposed to a Baal-religion for purely political reasons (cf. II Kings 10:31). As a right-wing patriot, he had probably headed up an increasingly powerful opposition party within Israel against Ahab's foreign religion, and was very anxious to gain favor with the "silent majority."

10. Israelites bearing tribute from Jehu, king of Israel, to Shalmaneser III, king of Assyria. It consists of silver, gold, vessels, buckets, a block of antimony, staves, and fruit. From the Black Obelisk. Courtesy, Inter-Varsity Fellowship.

This helps to explain Jehonadab's support of Jehu's drastic and ruthless policies. Jehonadab was the founder of a strict sect of Israelites (partly of Kenite extraction — I Chron. 2:55) who protested the corrupting influences of Canaanite culture by refusing wine and returning to the nomadic life of Israel's earlier days (cf. Jer. 35:1-11). He apparently was held in high respect by

---

[2]ANET, p. 277.

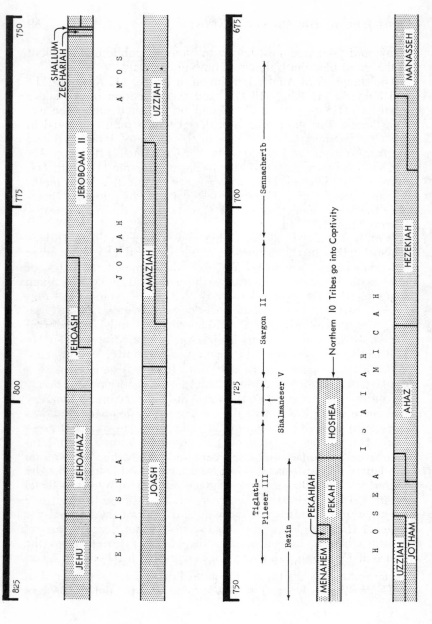

11. Time Chart: 825 to 675 B.C.

many, and Jehu was most happy to have his public endorsement of the great bloodbath that was now under way.

The slaughter of Ahab's henchmen in Jezreel (II Kings 10:11) and Samaria (II Kings 10:17), and the execution of Ahaziah's relatives (II Kings 10:12-14) would be expected under the circumstances. But the methods of deceit which Jehu employed in order to destroy Baal's followers in the Name of Jehovah reveal his true attitude and could never be condoned (II Kings 10: 18-28). God does not need human lies to promote His truth (cf. Rom. 3:7-8), nor can He honor those who feel that such methods are necessary for the accomplishment of His purposes (compare the tragic consequences of David's lie to the high priest — I Sam. 22:22).

With a diabolical efficiency that may be compared to Hitler's scheme of duping Jews into thinking that gas chambers were only shower rooms,[3] Jehu and Jehonadab jammed the house of Baal with his most zealous worshippers and then had them slaughtered. "Thus Jehu destroyed Baal out of Israel" (II Kings 10:28), carrying to completion the negative aspects of the life-long struggles of Elijah and Elisha. Ahab's family had refused the ministries and warnings of Jehovah's great prophets, so He sent to them a messenger they *would* understand.

For his zeal against this false deity, Jehu was honored with a dynasty that continued through four more generations and nearly a century (II Kings 10:30). But Jehu (like Nebuchadnezzar) was more of an instrument than a servant of Jehovah, and was spiritually incapable of promoting the true worship of Israel's God. Having destroyed Baal, he contented himself with Jeroboam's calf-cult at Bethel and Dan and "took no heed to walk in the law of Jehovah, the God of Israel, with all his heart: he departed not from the sins of Jeroboam, wherewith he made Israel to sin" (II Kings 10:31). Therefore, what he gained through zeal he lost through spiritual blindness, and Jehovah had to tell the prophet Hosea eighty years later to name his son Jezreel, "for yet a little while, and I will avenge the blood of Jezreel upon the house of Jehu, and will cause the kingdom of the house of Israel

---

[3]Cf. William L. Shirer, *The Rise and Fall of the Third Reich* (New York: Simon and Schuster, 1960), p. 970.

to cease" (Hos. 1:4). So the very deeds he supposedly performed for Jehovah (II Kings 10:16 — "Come with me and see my zeal for Jehovah") were an abomination to God because they were not done out of a Spirit-filled heart and for the glory of God.

Jehoahaz and Jehoash (II Kings 13:1–14:16)

In the very first year of his reign, Jehu, like other western kings, was forced to pay homage to Shalmaneser III of Assyria. Within a few years, however, Assyrian pressures were concentrated farther east, thus permitting Hazael of Damascus to begin his devastating campaigns against the entire trans-Jordan region (II Kings 10:32-33). Jehu had never fainted at the sight of blood; but he met his match in this scourge from Damascus, whose cruel treatment of Israelite captives brought tears to the prophet who anointed him and who foresaw his evil works (cf. II Kings 8:11-13).

Jehoahaz, the son of Jehu, was a religious carbon-copy of his father, bowing before the calf at Bethel which Jeroboam had set up. For this, Jehovah permitted Hazael to slash deep into his kingdom and decimate his army, leaving him only ten chariots (compared to Ahab's two thousand!). Perhaps the author of Kings was speaking ironically when he suggested further reading on Jehoahaz "and his might" (II Kings 13:8)!

When, in desperation, he temporarily abandoned his golden calf and turned directly to the Lord in prayer, God graciously "gave Israel a saviour, so that they went out from under the hand of the Syrians" (II Kings 13:5). But who was this "saviour"? It was either an unnamed general; or the son of Jehoahaz who "recovered the cities of Israel" (II Kings 13:25); or possibly even his grandson Jeroboam II ("he saved them by the hand of Jeroboam" — II Kings 14:27).

Jehoahaz was followed by another calf-worshipper named Joash (or Jehoash). He was notable for his bedside visit with the dying Elisha; for his three victories against Syria (II Kings 13:25); and for his complete victory over Amaziah, the "Thistle King" of Judah.[4] By now, it was becoming quite obvious that

----

[4]See pp. 105-106.

Jehu's "reforms" were almost totally worthless from a spiritual standpoint and that Satan was the unseen victor in the affairs of the northern kingdom.

Jeroboam II to Pekahiah (II Kings 14:23–15:26)

Jeroboam II may be considered as the greatest of the northern kings, even though he followed the spiritual pattern of his apostate fathers. During his long reign of forty-one years he succeeded in extending the borders of Israel far beyond Damascus, almost to the Euphrates, as God had promised Abraham (Gen. 15:18). Jeroboam's military successes were predicted by the prophet Jonah, who had doubtless returned by now from Nineveh (14:25). In fact, it may have been the repentance of the Ninevites that brought about a lull in Assyrian campaigns to the West during the reign of Jeroboam II, thus permitting him to move unchallenged deep into Syrian territory. Israel's prosperity during this era is clearly reflected in the writings of Hosea (12:8; 13:6), Amos (6:4-6), and Isaiah (28:1). But it was only a calm before the storm, for prosperity brought complacency, pride, and insensitivity to the voice of the Lord (Amos 7:10-13; cf. James 5:1-6).

The death of Jeroboam II in 753 B.C. was the beginning of the end for the northern kingdom. Within two years Zechariah his son died at the hand of an assassin (thus bringing a hasty fulfillment of God's promise of four generations of royal descendants to Jehu — II Kings 15:12); and the assassin himself (Shallum) was slain by an utterly calloused soldier named Menahem (II Kings 15:14; cf. vs. 16). Note the remarkable similarity of these events to those 130 years earlier, when Elah, after a two-year reign, was assassinated by Zimri, who in turn was brought to death a few days later by Omri. As in the final phase of the Roman Empire, one general after another seized the throne and the populace paid less and less heed to the bewildering game of intrigue, military takeover, and sham rule.

It was in the days of King Menahem that the dreadful spectre of Assyrian conquest loomed over the eastern horizon. For more than a generation Assyria had been relatively quiescent (a result of the ministry of Jonah in Nineveh?) with weak emperors such

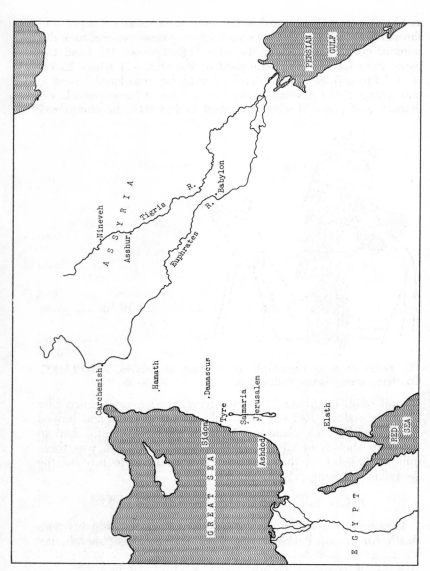

12. The Assyrian Empire.

as Shalmaneser IV, Ashurdan III, and Ashur-ninari V upon the throne. But in 745 B.C. an exceedingly vigorous general took the reins of government under the title Tiglathpileser III (and the name Pulu following his conquest of Babylon — II Kings 15:19; cf. I Chron. 5:26, where "and" should be translated "even"), and whipped the Assyrian army into a state of incomparable efficiency and zeal. Moving westward in 743 B.C., he conquered

13. Relief showing Tiglath-pileser III, king of Assyria, 745-727 B.C. Courtesy, Inter-Varsity Fellowship.

several small kingdoms. "As for Menahem, I overwhelmed him like a snowstorm and he . . . fled like a bird, alone, and bowed to my feet."[5] Sixty thousand Israelite "men of wealth" had to pay fifty shekels of silver each (a thousand talents was three million shekels), at the command of Menahem, to buy off the Assyrians (II Kings 15:20).

Pekah and Hoshea (II Kings 15:25–17:23)

Menahem's "dynasty" lasted only two years beyond his own death, for his son Pekahiah was slain by one of his generals, Pe-

---

[5]Pritchard, *ANET,* pp. 283-284.

kah the son of Remaliah. Furthermore, it appears that Pekah had already long since established himself as a pretender to the throne and a leader of the anti-Assyrian party especially in the trans-Jordan region of Gilead (II Kings 15:25), for he dated the beginning of his reign retroactively to the beginning of Mena-hem's.[6]

It was only a year after Pekah took the throne that King Uzziah of Judah died as a leper, and Isaiah saw the vision of Jehovah-Christ upon the throne of heaven (Isa. 6:1). With the powerful Uzziah now dead, Pekah began to exert great pressure upon Judah to join his western confederacy of anti-Assyrian states. But when Ahaz became co-regent with his politically weak father, Jotham, in Judah and refused to join, Pekah of Israel and Rezin of Syria invaded the southern kingdom, killed 120,000 soldiers and took 200,000 captives, who were soon released under threat of divine judgment (II Chron. 28:5-15). A few months later Pekah and Rezin plotted to replace Ahaz with a Phoenician puppet named Tabeel (Isa. 7:6), invaded Judah again[7] and "went up to Jerusalem to war against it, but could not prevail against it" (Isa. 7:1; cf. II Kings 16:5) because Ahaz had in the meantime succeeded in bribing Tiglath-pileser III to attack Damascus and northern Israel (II Kings 15:29; 16:7-9; II Chron. 28:20). Pekah and Rezin were now mere "tails of smoking firebrands" (Isa. 7:4) because Jehovah was not their Head (Isa. 7:7-9).

Thus, the great darkness of Assyrian deportation fell first upon the land of Galilee (cf. Isa. 9:1). Utterly terrified by the prospect of total collapse under the iron fist of Tiglath-pileser III, the majority of Israelites now backed Hoshea's plot to remove Pekah and to come to terms with Assyria. As the great conqueror explained it: "They overthrew their king Pekah and I placed Hoshea as king over them. I received from them ten talents of gold, 1,000 talents of silver as their tribute, and brought them to Assyria."[8]

---

[6]Thiele, *Mysterious Numbers,* pp. 123-124.

[7]Cf. Edward J. Young, *Studies in Isaiah* (Wm. B. Eerdmans Publishing Co., 1954), pp. 145-151.

[8]Pritchard, *ANET,* p. 284.

In spite of the fact that Hoshea was the least wicked of the northern kings (II Kings 17:2), the kingdom collapsed anyway, thus demonstrating that it was rotten beyond recovery. Five years after Hoshea became king, Tiglath-pileser III died, and the new Assyrian emperor, Shalmaneser V, demanded a continuation of the heavy tribute. However, the burden became unbearable and Hoshea apparently was forced by his leaders to seek out an alliance with the Egyptians. Such treachery was, of course, intolerable to the Assyrians, who promptly imprisoned Hoshea and began a long siege of the well-fortified capital city of Samaria (724-722 B.C.). Just as the siege ended, Shalmaneser V died, and his successor, Sargon II (cf. Isa. 20:1) completed the destruction of the city and the deportation of its inhabitants: "At the beginning of my royal rule I conquered the town of the Samarians. . . . I led away as prisoners 27,290 inhabitants of it and equipped from among them soldiers to man 50 chariots for my royal corps. . . . The town I rebuilt better than it was before and settled therein people from countries which I myself had conquered. I placed an officer of mine as governor over them and imposed upon them tribute as is customary for Assyrian citizens."[9] Before the days of Tiglath-pileser III, Assyrian monarchs had been content to raid western countries and exact tribute from them. But now a drastic new method of shattering national morale and resistance was instituted — mass deportations of peoples from one end of the empire to the other. God had indeed prepared a "rod of his anger" to send against "a profane nation" (Isa. 10:5-6).

So tragic and shocking was this catastrophe that the author of Kings paused in the midst of his narrative to list about twenty reasons why God's judgment was so richly deserved (II Kings 17:7-18). God was not helpless to rescue Israel from her enemies. In fact, He was the One who raised them up and brought them to destroy His people. Nor had He broken His covenant promises to the nation; for a remnant of each of the northern tribes had long since fled to the tribe of Judah to perpetuate their identity there (cf. II Chron. 11:16; Acts 26:7; James 1:1; and the reference to Anna "of the tribe of Asher" in Luke 2:36).

---

[9]Pritchard, *ANET,* p. 284.

14. Limestone relief of Sargon II, king of Assyria, from the palace at Khorsabad.

15. One of the colossal human-headed winged bulls that guarded the entrance to the palace of Sargon II at Khorsabad. Courtesy, Oriental Institute.

We may imagine his tears falling upon the parchment as the author of Kings penned Israel's epitaph: "So Israel was carried away out of their own land to Assyria unto this day" (II Kings 17:23). And the tragedy was compounded because Judah refused to learn spiritual lessons from the experience of her sister kingdom to the north (II Kings 17:19; cf. Ezek. 16:46-59), thus explaining why the author of Kings was himself in far off Babylon when he completed his book (cf. II Kings 25:27-30).

The Destruction of Israel (II Kings 17:24-41)

Isaiah had predicted that the process of deporting Israelites and importing foreigners with the consequent destruction of the ethnic identity of the northern kingdom (and the formation of a new mongrel race called Samaritans) would take sixty-five years beginning in 734 B.C. (Isa. 7:8). Thus, "the king of Assyria" in II Kings 17:24 who completed this monumental task must have been Esarhaddon, the grandson of Sargon, whose reign ended in 669 B.C., exactly sixty-five years after Isaiah's prophecy. This is confirmed by the fact that the Samaritan half-breeds who hindered the work of Zerubbabel and Joshua in rebuilding the Jerusalem temple insisted that "we sacrifice unto him since the days of Esar-haddon king of Assyria, who brought us up hither" (Ezra 4:2).

It is noteworthy that so many Israelites vanished from the scene during those years that lions began to multiply beyond control. God had long since warned the nation: "If ye walk contrary to me . . . I will send the beast of the field among you, which shall rob you of your children, and destroy your cattle, and make you few in number; and your ways shall become desolate" (Lev. 26:21-22; cf. Exod. 23:29). Having utterly rejected the mild warnings of two she-bears in the days of Elisha (cf. II Kings 2:24), the land was now literally overrun with thousands of lions.

To meet this crisis, the new inhabitants called for a Jehovah calf-priest to be returned to Bethel to "teach them the law of the god of the land" (II Kings 17:27). The priest, however, must have felt somewhat hindered in his teaching ministry, for the golden calf had been carried away from Bethel to Assyria:

"The inhabitants of Samaria shall be in terror for the calves of Beth-aven; for the people thereof shall mourn over it . . . because it is departed from it. It also shall be carried unto Assyria . . ." (Hos. 10:5-6).

If this priest set as his goal the mere perpetuation of the name of Jehovah in the northern regions he succeeded marvelously well. But the *worship* of Jehovah, even in the style of Jeroboam I, vanished permanently in the north (II Kings 17:34). Each group of importees from Babylon, Cuth, Hamath, Avva, and Sepharvaim (from various extremities of the Fertile Crescent — II Kings 17:24, 30, 31) maintained their basic loyalty to their own gods, and either added Jehovah to the already crowded pantheon or perhaps called their favorite god by the name of the local deity, Jehovah, whom they sought to placate by this means. "They feared Jehovah, and served their own gods, after the manner of the nations from among whom they had been carried away" (II Kings 17:33).

This was the final fruit of Jeroboam's break with Jerusalem and Judah: a stench in the nostrils of God and man. From this time onward, the southern Jews had "no dealings with the Samaritans" (John 4:9); and though the Samaritan people continue to the present hour, their numbers have dwindled to a mere handful and their national glory has departed forever.

Chapter 9

FROM JEHOSHAPHAT TO HEZEKIAH

Jehoram and Ahaziah of Judah (II Chron. 21—22)

The fruits of Jehoshaphat's alliance with wicked Ahab and Jezebel of Israel (through the marriage of his son Jehoram to their daughter Athaliah) now became clearly evident. As is often the case with children, young Jehoram copied the weaknesses of his father but not his strengths, and not only entered willingly into a marriage relationship with the northern princess, but accepted wholeheartedly the pagan ways of her parents as well. Thus Queen Jezebel controlled both her husband and her daughter's husband, and through them permeated both Israel and Judah with the poisonous leaven of Baalism.

As soon as his father was dead, Jehoram eliminated his six younger and more righteous brothers (II Chron. 21:2-4; cf. vs. 13) to whom their father had given many gifts and fortified cities in Judah (II Chron. 21:3). This was doubtless at the instigation of his wife Athaliah (21:6; 22:3), even as Jezebel had engineered the murder of Naboth and his sons at Jezreel. Jehoram's brothers, along with some of the nobility, apparently had sought to hinder his plan to introduce the outright worship of Baal in Judah (cf. II Chron. 23:17), and lost their lives as a result. Were these men true believers? Did they bear a consistent witness to Jehovah in those evil days? One of the great blessings of heaven will be a personalized study of the unabridged edition of God's Hall of Fame.

God's response to Jehoram's depraved and outrageous acts was drastic. First, He permitted Edom and Libnah to slip out of Judah's hand (II Chron. 21:8-10), even as Moab had earlier revolted from Israel (II Kings 3:5). Second, He permitted Philistines and Arabians to invade Judah, sack Jerusalem, and carry away the king's wives and sons, with the exception of Athaliah and Jehoahaz (or Ahaziah).[1] Third, He directed Elijah, His special witness against Baal-worshippers, to write a letter to Jehoram, warning him of a horrible form of dysentery that would come upon him (II Chron. 21:12-15), which brought him to an untimely grave two years later. Fourth, Jehoram was deprived of an honorable burial. "His people made no burning for him like the burnings of his father [cf. II Chron. 16:14 for Asa] . . . and he departed without being desired; and they buried him in the city of David, but not in the sepulchres of the kings" (II Chron. 21:19-20). Thus did Jehovah permit Satan's man to have his little day in the sun, and then cast him forth "like an abominable branch. . . . thou shalt not be joined with them in burial, because thou hast destroyed thy land, thou hast slain thy people; the seed of evildoers shall not be named forever" (Isa. 14: 19-20, concerning Satan's future tool, the Antichrist).

Ahaziah, Jehoram's son and successor, was, if possible, even more wicked than his father; but he was cut off before the end of his first year and therefore had less opportunity to display his depravity. His mother, Athaliah, not only named him after her evil brother in the north, but "was his counsellor to do wickedly" (II Chron. 22:3). Furthermore, "the house of Ahab . . . were his counsellors after the death of his father, to his destruction. He walked also after their counsel" (II Chron. 22: 3-5). A more discouraging background for a Davidic king can hardly be imagined!

But Satan overreached himself when he bound Ahaziah so closely to Ahab's family, for God's appointed hour for the destruction of that dynasty had come. While Ahaziah was in Jezreel visiting his wounded uncle Jehoram, Jehu, the scourge of God, swept in from the eastern battlefront and killed the Israelite king. Horrified by what he saw Ahaziah fled by way of the garden house (II Kings 9:27) southward to Samaria. There he

---

[1]It was at this time, apparently, that Obadiah denounced Edom for standing "on the other side, in the day that strangers carried away his (Jerusalem's) substance, and foreigners entered into his gates, and cast lots upon Jerusalem" (Obad. 11). Such an early date for Obadiah is suggested by the fact that Jeremiah (49:14-16) seems to quote from him, and not the reverse. For supporting arguments, see Gleason Archer, *A Survey of Old Testament Introduction* (Moody Press, 1964), pp. 287-91.

was captured, and brought in his chariot to Ibleam, halfway back to Jezreel, where Jehu ordered him to be killed (II Chron. 22: 9). However, the blow was not immediately fatal, and Ahaziah managed to escape westward up the ascent of Gur toward Megiddo where he finally died (II Kings 9:27).[2] While his body was being returned to Jerusalem for burial, forty-two of his cousins, who had somehow succeeded in escaping the slaughter inflicted upon their family by Philistines and Arabians (II Chron. 21:16-17), were intercepted and killed by Jehu on their way to visit the royal family in Jezreel (II Kings 10:12-14).

Queen Athaliah (II Chron. 22:10—23:15)

Satan, knowing that his time was short, stirred up Athaliah, his feminine Antichrist in Jerusalem, and "she arose and destroyed all the seed royal of the house of Judah" (II Chron. 22:10). The real surprise here is that there was anyone left for her to kill! In the marvellous providence of God, a baby son of Ahaziah was rescued by his aunt, Jehosheba, whose husband Jehoiada "just happened to be" the high priest at that time. Hiding him first in a bedchamber and then in the Temple, they managed to prevent the queen (or anyone else) from knowing of his existence for six long years!

What must God's people have thought about God's promise to David: "Thy house and thy kingdom shall be made sure for ever before thee: thy throne shall be established for ever" (II Sam. 7:16)? Did some attempt to spiritualize the promise in the light of its apparent failure of fulfillment? Those who did were guilty of underestimating the Word of their God, for the literal interpretation of the prophecy had its vindication in a Temple playroom. Even more complex for God's people was the problem of Jeremiah's curse upon the line of Jehoiachin (Jer. 22: 28-30) two centuries later. After Jehoiachin's death, where was the legitimate Davidic king? The answer was hidden in the genetic code of a woman who came from one of David's non-cursed lines (Nathan — II Sam. 5:14; Luke 3:31), whose virgin-

---

[2]See the map depicting these movements in Aharoni, *The Macmillan Bible Atlas* (New York: The Macmillan Co., 1968), p. 85.

born Son could be adopted by a descendant of Jehoiachin (Joseph of Nazareth), thereby transmitting to this child the legal right to the throne without at the same time transmitting the curse! Truly, God's ways and thoughts are higher than ours, even as the heavens are higher than the earth (Isa. 55:9).

In the seventh year of Judah's tribulation period under Athaliah, the fulness of God's time finally came. The high priest Jehoiada secretly summoned to the Temple five faithful captains with the Carites,[3] plus representative Levites and other godly leaders, and after making them take an oath of loyalty, showed them the crown prince. The experience must have been electrifying. There *was* a king in Judah! God's promises had *not* been frustrated by Satan! Thus, Jehoiada reminded them: "Behold, the king's son shall reign, as Jehovah hath spoken concerning the sons of David" (II Chron. 23:3).

Waiting until a Sabbath day, when more Temple workers would be present, Jehoiada divided the incoming shift of priests and Levites into three groups to guard strategic points, while the outgoing group, instead of going to their homes, stayed in the Temple to protect the king (II Chron. 23:8). The fact that all of this could be planned without the queen's knowledge shows how feeble her popular support really was by now.

Armed with David's weapons, the defenders of David's dynasty brought forth David's descendant, placed the crown upon him, presented to him a copy of God's Law (cf. Deut. 17:18-20), anointed him, and shouted, "Long live the king!!" Even as Adonijah heard too late the shouting at his brother Solomon's coronation (I Kings 1:41-53), so Athaliah found herself an unwilling spectator at her own abdication. Instead of panicking like Adonijah, however, she followed the example of her mother Jezebel and faced her enemies with fierce boldness, screaming "Treason! treason!" These were her last recorded words; for in just retribution for her blasphemies and murders, she was maneuvered away from God's house which her sons had ransacked (II Chron. 24:7) and was slain near the palace.

---

[3]The Carites were probably the "Cherethites" of II Sam. 8:18, who, along with the Pelethites and Gittites, were Philistine mercenary troops who were fiercely loyal to David and the Davidic dynasty (II Sam. 15: 18; cf. I Sam. 30:14, Ezek. 25:16, Zeph. 2:5).

Thus ended the dynasty of Omri in its Judean extension, just seven years after its northern extension had been destroyed by Jehu. The mopping-up operations were quickly accomplished; for the people covenanted to serve Jehovah, and then destroyed Baal's temple, altars, images, and priest[4] without having to employ Jehu's deceptive methods at all (cf. II Kings 10:18-28).

Joash, the Boy King (II Kings 12; II Chron. 24)

The forty-year reign of Joash may be divided into two parts — before and after the death of his spiritual guardian, Jehoiada. The statement that "Joash did that which was right in the eyes of Jehovah *all the days of Jehoiada the priest*" is ominous. Without the moral and spiritual courage of this high priest, Joash was as unstable as Lot without Abram. Therefore, God showed His mercy to the people of Judah by extending Jehoiada's life to an amazing 130 years![5]

One worthy project that Joash accomplished during the first phase of his reign was the repair of the Temple. At first glance, II Kings 12:4-6 seems to imply that it took the priests twenty-three years to collect money for repairing the Temple! However, the text does not state how long before his twenty-third year the project was started. There may be some hint of dishonesty among the priests or their "acquaintance" (II Kings 12:5, 7 — possibly money changers or assessors) in handling the offerings. At any rate, a voluntary offering system with a "Joash chest" proved more effective, and the precious metals (coinage had not yet been invented) were turned over to faithful workers who completed all the necessary repairs.

Then came Phase Two of the reign of Joash, and with it great tragedies. With Jehoiada dead, a group of left-wing no-

---

[4]The name of this priest, Mattan, may be an abbreviation for Mattan-baal ("gift of Baal"), just as Mattaniah meant "gift of Jehovah" (cf. II Kings 24:17).

[5]II Chron. 24:15. Thus, Jehoiada lived longer than anyone on record during the previous thousand years, since Amram, an ancestor of Moses died at 137 (Exod. 6:20). We are disappointed, however, to see Jehoiada's concession to human frailty in giving two wives to young Joash (II Chron. 24:3).

bles caught the ear of the king and turned him from the Lord
so completely that he actually commanded his men to stone
Zechariah, the son of Jehoiada, for speaking out against the new
apostasy. As the faithful prophet lay dying in the Temple court,
he cried out: "Jehovah look upon it and require it" (II Chron.
24:22).[6] And Jehovah *did* require it of Joash, for before the
year was over, Hazael's army approached Jerusalem from the
west, defeated the Judean army (II Chron. 24:23-24), and was
finally bought off with Temple treasures (II Kings 12:18). Joash himself was sorely wounded, and was later slain by two
conspirators. The supreme indignity came when he was denied
burial among the sepulchres of the kings, though Jehoiada was
given this special honor (II Chron. 24:15, 25).

Amaziah, the "Thistle King" (II Kings 14; II Chron. 25)

Amaziah's reign began well, with a wise handling of an emo-
tionally-charged situation. Most ancient kings would have wiped
out the entire family of an assassin to prevent further retalia-
tion. But Amaziah entrusted this matter to the Lord and obeyed
the Scriptures (II Chron. 25:4; cf. Deut. 24:16). Furthermore,
he obeyed God's prophet by sending home 100,000 Ephraimite
mercenaries, even though the hundred talents of silver had already been given to them and their humiliation would doubtless
cause them to retaliate (II Chron. 25:5-10, 13). It is obvious
that Judah's army had not yet recovered from the disastrous defeat in the days of Joash (cf. II Chron. 24:24), and therefore
additional troops were needed for the campaign against Edom.
But it is also true that spiritual principles had to take prece-
dence over military ones; and not only was God able to give
Amaziah a great victory over Edom without the Ephraimite
soldiers (II Chron. 25:10-12), but He was also able to more
than make up for the great financial loss (II Chron. 25:9).

That Amaziah should bow down and burn incense to the
Edomite idols which were obviously not able to deliver even

---

[6]Many believe that Jesus referred to this event in Matthew 23:35. However, he spoke of "Zachariah son of Barachiah" who was a postexilic
prophet (Zech. 1:1). The situation may have been quite similar. See
J. Barton Payne, "Zachariah Who Perished," *Grace Journal* (Fall, 1967).

their own people (II Chron. 25:14-15) is so ridiculous as to be almost unbelievable. But how believable or rational is *any* sin? Not until the mind of man has surrendered to the Lord can it even begin to function properly (cf. Luke 8:35 — "in his right mind at the feet of Jesus"). So Amaziah had to be rebuked by God and suffer terribly in order that he (and we) might learn the folly of spiritual disobedience.

Idolatry clouded his mind so completely that instead of obeying God's prophet as he had done before the battle (II Chron. 25:10), he denounced him with bitter words: "Have we made thee of the king's counsel? forbear: why shouldest thou be smitten?" (II Chron. 25:16). God prevented him from actually smiting the prophet (as Asa and Joash had done in their moments of rebellion against God); but the thought was as bad as the deed, and even more alarming words came back upon his head: "I know that God hath determined to destroy thee, because thou hast done this, and hast not hearkened unto my counsel" (II Kings 25:16).

All of this necessary background information to the disastrous battle with Joash of Israel is omitted by the author of Kings, who assumed that his readers were aware of the existence of at least this portion of the book of Chronicles.[7]

Doubtless Amaziah was able to convince his people that the war was necessary for the sake of national honor; but this time Jehovah was not with him (II Chron. 25:20). Supremely confident of his invincible power after (1) defeating the Edomites completely, (2) capturing and then enlisting the help of their gods, and (3) silencing Jehovah's meddlesome prophet, Amaziah challenged the king of Israel to a military contest in revenge for the damaging border raids by the malcontent mercenaries whom he had previously rejected at Jehovah's insistence (II Chron. 25:13). But the king of Israel, astounded at Amaziah's ambitious pride, cut him down to size with a well-phrased fable: A worthless and despicable thistle once tried to

---

[7]Similarly, the author of Kings omitted the reason for Baasha's fortification of Ramah (I Kings 15:17) because the full story was available in II Chron. 15:9 ff. More frequently, however, the Chronicler assumes the reader's knowledge of the book of Kings.

put himself on a par with stately cedar trees until a passing
beast accidently stepped on him, and his ambitious plans came
to a sudden end![8] In other words, O Amaziah, pitiful "thistle
king" of Judah, stay in your own league and be content with
the little trophies you have already won, lest you and your kingdom should come to disaster!

But Amaziah did not discern God's voice through the fable;
and thus suffered a staggering defeat at Beth-shemesh (just
west of Jerusalem), saw six hundred feet of the northern wall
of his capital city broken down, and lost hostages as well as Temple treasures (II Chron. 25:21-24). Furthermore, Amaziah
henceforth lost the confidence of his people; Uzziah his son was
made co-regent while still a teen-ager; and conspirators finally
succeeded in killing Amaziah at Lachish.

King Uzziah, the Leper (II Chron. 26)

The story of king Uzziah, or "Azariah" as his name is spelled
in the book of Kings, is remarkably similar to that of Asa, Joash, and Amaziah. Running well in the beginning, each of these
kings became preoccupied with their own success and prosperity (which God gave them in the first place) and were sorely
chastened with disease, military defeat, and (in the case of Uzziah) leprosy. "He that thinketh he standeth, let him take heed
lest he fall" (I Cor. 10:12).

The tremendous influence which God's prophets had upon
their contemporaries may be judged by this statement concerning king Uzziah: "he set himself to seek God in the days of
Zechariah, who had understanding in the vision of God: and as
long as he sought Jehovah, God made him to prosper" (II Chron.
26:5). We know nothing of this prophet Zechariah (possibly
named after the one whom Uzziah's grandfather had commanded to be stoned), but his influence upon both king and
kingdom may be compared to that of Jehoiada the high priest
in the early years of Joash. In a real sense, therefore, all of Uzziah's great achievements during these early years of his long
reign (defeating enemy nations; building cities, towers, and

---

[8]The only other fable in the Bible was uttered by Jotham, a son of
Gideon, concerning trees that sought for a king (Judges 9:8-15).

cisterns; raising cattle and fruit trees; equipping his army with the "latest" weapons) can be attributed to Zechariah who encouraged the king to "seek God." Thus, Uzziah "waxed exceeding strong" (II Chron. 26:8) and "was marvellously helped" (II Chron. 26:15).

All of this is the background for one of the greatest falls in Old Testament history. The similarity to Satan's fall from heaven is striking: "when he was strong, his heart was lifted up" (II Chron. 26:16).[9] But why did Uzziah desire to "burn incense upon the altar of incense"? Because he was no longer satisfied with being a mere king, and desired to be a "divine king" like some of his contemporaries, especially in Egypt.[10] But the depth of this sin can only be measured by the sacredness of the position he was usurping, namely, the position of the great Priest-King, our Lord Jesus Christ who alone is qualified to sit at God's right hand as "a priest for ever after the order of Melchizedek" (Ps. 110:1, 4), indeed, as "a priest upon his throne" (Zech. 6:13). It was God's revealed plan that no Aaronic priest should ever sit upon David's throne (cf. Gen. 49:10; Heb. 7:14), and no descendant of David should ever be an Aaronic priest. Uzziah clearly understood this clear distinction between kings and priests in Israel and thus was guilty of deliberately defying God.

With great moral courage, Azariah the high priest and eighty priests with him confronted Uzziah and denounced him in the name of the Lord. The moment he responded with anger instead of repentance, leprosy broke out on his forehead,[11] and

---

[9]Cf. Isa. 14:13 — "thou saidst in thy heart, I will ascend into heaven"; and Ezek. 28:17 — "Thy heart was lifted up because of thy beauty." Thus, the New Testament pastor was not to be a novice, "lest being puffed up he fall into the condemnation of the devil" (I Tim. 3:6).

[10]It is possible that Uzziah wanted to be another Melchizedek (Gen. 14:18). Jeroboam I similarly attempted to combine royal and priestly functions in himself (cf. I Kings 12:27-33).

[11]Miriam was similarly punished for intruding into the God-given authority of Moses. The verb "spake" in Numbers 12:1 is feminine! For excellent discussions of leprosy, see McClintock and Strong, *Cyclopedia of Biblical Theological and Ecclesiastical Literature*, Vol. V (Grand Rapids: Baker Book House, reprinted 1969); and Patrick Feeny, *The Fight Against Leprosy* (New York: American Leprosy Missions, Inc., 1964).

in great terror the king rushed out of the Temple, followed by eighty-one priests urging him onward. The final decade of his life was spent in a separate place crying out "Unclean, unclean" to all who passed by (cf. Lev. 13:45-46). A more tragic end to an otherwise glorious reign can hardly be imagined. But from a broader aspect, Uzziah symbolized the condition of the entire nation before God. As Isaiah the prophet confessed when he saw the Holy One of Israel in the year that king Uzziah died, "Woe is me! for I am undone; because I am a man of unclean lips, and I dwell in the midst of a people of unclean lips" (Isa. 6:5).

Jotham and Ahaz (II Chron. 27–28)

Very little is written about King Jotham in Scripture, possibly because his reign was overlapped largely by co-regencies with his father, Uzziah, and son, Ahaz. Though he was a godly man, his reign was somewhat colorless. He built some cities and towers, and won a foreign war (which is not mentioned in Kings). The only significant adverse comment is that "he entered not into the temple of Jehovah" (II Chron. 27:2). Was he trying to honor his father who was smitten with leprosy in the Temple, or was he superstitiously fearful of suffering the same fate? Nevertheless, "Jotham was mighty because he ordered his ways before Jehovah his God" (II Chron. 27:6).

Ahaz was a shocking contrast to his godly father. In fact, he ranks among the most wicked rulers of the southern kingdom, in a class with such blots on the Biblical record as Jehoram, Athaliah, Manasseh, Jehoiakim, and Zedekiah. His personal contribution to the record of royal depravity was to burn alive some of his own children as sacrifices to the god Molech, setting an example which Manasseh later followed (II Chron. 28:3; 33:6; cf. Lev. 18:21). God's response to this was to permit an Ephraimite to kill another of his sons (II Chron. 28:7), so that when Hezekiah finally became king he had no brothers to challenge him.

This was a time of great turmoil in Palestine, as Assyrian armies under the brilliant leadership of Tiglathpileser III repeatedly crushed these small western kingdoms with burdens of tribute and threats of mass deportation. Pekah of Israel was launched to the throne on a wave of anti-Assyrian feeling, and he determined to bring Judah into his western confederacy.[12] When Judah, now ruled by Ahaz, refused to cooperate, Pekah of Israel and Rezin of Damascus invaded their southern neighbor and carried off many captives to Samaria and Damascus (II Chron. 28:5-15). While in Damascus as a captive, Ahaz sacrificed to the gods that smote him. "But they were the ruin of him and of all Israel" (II Chron. 28:23).

After his release, and the release of 200,000 of his citizens from Samaria, Ahaz was attacked by Edomites from the southeast and Philistines from the west. Furthermore, Israel and Syria prepared to invade Judah again (Isa. 7:1, II Kings 16:5). Jehovah offered to encourage his faith with a spectacular sign (Isa. 7:11), but with mock piety Ahaz brushed this gracious offer to one side: "I will not ask, neither will I tempt Jehovah" (Isa. 7:12).

Thus, rejecting all of God's warnings through Isaiah, Ahaz followed through with his desperate plan of bribing Tiglathpileser III to attack Damascus and Israel. He may have justified this move by appealing to Asa's example (who hired Ben-hadad of Syria to attack Baasha of Israel), but Isaiah warned him that he was playing with fire and that the Assyrian would ultimately destroy Judah also (Isa. 7:17—8:8). Ahaz received a foretaste of this in his own lifetime, for "Tiglathpileser king of Assyria came unto him, and distressed him, but strengthened him not" (II Chron. 28:20). The more he gave to Tiglathpileser the more was demanded of him, until he had to strip the Temple and his own palace to make payments, "but it helped him not" (II Chron. 28:21).

It was not that Ahaz neglected Tiglathpileser. In fact, as soon as the Assyrians conquered Syria (732 B.C.), the Judean king hurried to Damascus to pay his personal respects to the great king (II Kings 16:10). While there, he saw the great altar that Tiglathpileser erected for the glory of Asshur, sent for Urijah the priest to copy and duplicate it, and hastened to demonstrate his loyalty to his Assyrian overlords by worshipping exclusively at

---

[12]For a discussion of Pekah's policies, see p. 94.

this replica within the Temple court in Jerusalem. He even set Jehovah's altar to one side (II Kings 16:10-16), made other drastic changes in Temple arrangements "because of the king of Assyria" (II Kings 16:18), and finally "cut in pieces the vessels of the house of God and shut up the doors of the house of Jehovah" (II Chron. 28:24).

But if Ahaz thought he could gain a solid and lasting friendship with Assyria by such means, he was utterly mistaken. He was now in the "big leagues" of international intrigue and political depravity, where truth, honesty, faithfulness, and love were unknown entities. Having deliberately abandoned Jehovah, he and his little kingdom (the remaining refuge for God's people in the world) were now hopelessly enmeshed in Satan's web. "Forasmuch as this people have refused the waters of Shiloah that go softly . . . the Lord bringeth upon them the waters of the River, strong and many, even the king of Assyria, and all his glory . . . and it shall sweep onward into Judah . . . and the stretching out of its wings shall fill the breadth of thy land, O Immanuel" (Isa. 8:6-8).

Ahaz died and was buried in dishonor. And such would have been the fate of his kingdom too were it not for Hezekiah his son, whose faith in Jehovah in an hour of ultimate crisis was God's reason for extending the nation's existence yet another hundred years.

Chapter 10

HEZEKIAH AND THE ASSYRIANS

The Great Revival (II Kings 18:1-8)

With the probable exception of Josiah, who lived a hundred years later, Hezekiah was the most godly descendant of David ever to sit upon the throne (II Kings 18:5; cf. 23:25). His reign began with a great revival of true religion in Judah, the effects of which reached even to the northern tribal territories (II Chron. 30:5-27).

From a negative standpoint, there was much destruction and removal of the symbols of pagan idolatry that had accummulated during his father's reign (II Kings 18:4; cf. II Chron. 31:1). Among the things destroyed was the *brazen serpent* which Moses had made in the wilderness seven hundred years earlier (Num. 21:8, 9)! Instead of serving as a reminder of the blessed truth that salvation comes by obedient faith in God's promises (cf. John 3:14, 15), the famous relic had become an idol before which men bowed and offered incense! Therefore the young king did to it what we should be prepared to do to *anything* that positions itself between us and God — see it for what it really is (Nehushtan — a mere "piece of brass," ASV margin), and *destroy* it! So it was that Paul's converts at Ephesus saw their books on magical arts in a new light, gathered them into a huge pile, and "burned them in the sight of all . . . so mightily grew the word of the Lord and prevailed" (Acts 19:19, 20). "My little children," wrote an aged apostle, "guard yourselves from idols" (I John 5:21).

From a positive standpoint, Hezekiah opened the temple doors which Ahaz his father had closed (II Chron. 29:3; cf. 28:24), commissioned the priests and Levites to cleanse the temple (II Chron. 29:4-19), offered appropriate sacrifices (II Chron. 29:20-36), planned a special Passover which had to be delayed one month because so few were ceremonially qualified (II Chron. 30:1-4), and invited people from every tribe, not only from the south, but also from the northern areas that had suffered the loss

111

of their king and capital city a few years earlier (II Chron. 30: 5-12).

Tribute to Sennacherib (II Kings 18:13-16)

It is apparent that Hezekiah did not fully count the cost in one decision he made during the early years of revival and reformation: "he rebelled against the king of Assyria, and served him not" (II Kings 18:7). This was not a particularly courageous act at the time, for the Assyrian army was preoccupied in the eastern part of the empire for several years, and Sargon II died in 705 B.C. But now the picture had changed drastically. In 701 B.C., Sennacherib, having consolidated the empire and reorganized the army following the death of his father, moved westward to punish various kings, including Hezekiah, and to force them once again to pay heavy annual tributes to Nineveh.[1]

Hezekiah was utterly terrified at this sudden and unexpected confrontation with the mighty Assyrian army, and therefore allowed himself to be caught in a trap of his own making. "The fear of man bringeth a snare, but whoso putteth his truth in Jehovah shall be safe" (Prov. 29:25). Instead of trusting God, he asked for terms of peace, which is exactly what any worldly ruler would have done under the circumstances (cf. I Kings 20:4). In the words of our Lord, "what king, as he goeth to encounter another king in war, will not sit down first and take counsel whether he is able with ten thousand to meet him that cometh against him with twenty thousand? Or else, while the other is yet a great way off, he sendeth an ambassage, and asketh conditions of peace" (Luke 14:31, 32). The tribute imposed upon Judah was enormous (nearly $2,000,000), and Hezekiah had to empty both the temple and palace treasuries, and even to strip the gold from the doors and pillars of the temple (II Kings 18:16).[2]

---

[1] In a clay prism, Sennacherib lists the following familiar cities and countries which were conquered and forced to pay tribute during the 701 B.C. campaign: Sidon, Arvad, Byblos, Ammon, Moab, Edom, Ashdod, Ashkelon, Ekron, and Joppa (*ANET*, pp. 287, 288).

[2] In anticipation of Sennacherib's next move, Hezekiah had a tunnel cut under Mt. Zion to bring the water of Gihon spring into the city (cf. II Kings 20:20, II Chron. 32:3, 4, 30; and for the inscription cut into the wall of the tunnel, *ANET*, p. 321.)

16. The Siloam Tunnel cut by Hezekiah (2 Kings 20:20). This 1,750-foot conduit brought the waters of the Spring Gihon inside the city of Jerusalem. Courtesy, Matson Photo Service.

Sennacherib's First Threat (II Kings 18:17-37)

His appetite whetted by Hezekiah's easy surrender to his demands, Sennacherib determined to take everything (compare the effort of France and England to appease Hitler by giving him the outer borders of Czechoslovakia in 1938). It was very important to the Assyrian commander to eliminate Jerusalem as a potential threat on his left flank as he faced the Egyptian army to the south. Therefore he sent three highly trained military ambassadors to terrify the Jews of Jerusalem into immediate surrender: *Tartan* ("Field Marshal"; cf. Isa. 20:1), *Rab-saris* ("Chief Eunuch"; cf. Jer. 39:3), and *Rabshakeh* ("Chief Officer").

The location of the confrontation was significant: "the conduit of the upper pool, which is in the highway of the fuller's field" (II Kings 18:17). It was here, on the high ground overlooking the city from the northwest, where laundrymen (fullers) found sufficient water for their trade, that Isaiah had challenged wicked Ahaz thirty-three years earlier with a divine alternative: either trust Jehovah or face the Assyrians (Isa. 7:3-17). Ahaz, on behalf of his people, made his decision, and God's warning was now being fulfilled.

Hezekiah sent Eliakim, Shebnah, and Joah to meet the three Assyrian ambassadors. But instead of discussing the matter privately, Rabshakeh insisted on using the occasion as a means of terrifying the curious Jews who were crowded along the walls of the city (II Kings 18:26; cf. II Chron. 32:18). Not only did he shout at them with a loud voice, but he also spoke in Hebrew so he could be clearly understood. Does this mean that he went to the trouble of learning Hebrew, or did he speak through an interpreter? The Jewish delegation begged him to speak to them in Aramaic, the commerical and diplomatic language of the Fertile Crescent (which by this time was replacing the more cumbersome Akkadian language). He not only refused to do so, but insulted the people of the city (II Kings 18:27). In our own day, the utter frustration and futility of engaging in "peace talks" with Communist leaders comes vividly to mind by way of comparison.

Rabshakeh used six arguments to pressure the Jews into the immediate surrender of their city. The first, third, and fifth were mundane and practical reasons; but the second, fourth, and sixth were religious and theological in character. The *first argument* was actually quite valid: Egypt was an undependable and weak reed to lean upon as far as military alliance was concerned. Isaiah the prophet had repeatedly warned the Jews against heeding the pro-Egyptian party in Judah, which tended to grow in influence whenever pressure from Assyria increased (Isa. 30:2, 5, 7; 31:1). The people of Judah had already seen what happened to the northern kingdom when Hoshea "sent messengers to So king of Egypt" (II Kings 17:4), and not only received no help from him but thereby provoked the ultimate wrath of his Assyrian overlord (a century later king Zedekiah tried the same tactic and failed, too — Jer. 37:5-10). Rabshakeh didn't realize, however, that the real reason why Egypt was no help to Israel was that God blocked any alternative to trusting in Him.

The *second argument,* a theological one, must have seemed laughable to most of the listening Jews. Hezekiah had removed all the "Jehovah altars" throughout the land (II Kings 18:4; cf. II Chron. 31:1), and destroyed Moses' brazen serpent (II Kings 18:4). Sure, then, the Assyrians insisted, the Jews could no longer count on any help from Jehovah, whose honor and glory had thus been reduced by Hezekiah's fanatical inconoclasm! Such reasoning might have seemed impressive to idolaters who thought that the size and number of idols erected in honor of a particular deity would be a valid measuring-stick of the amount of blessing that could be expected from him; but even the average Jew could see through such religious logic (cf. Isa. 10:10, 11).

Rabshakeh's *third argument* was simply that the Assyrian army was overwhelmingly large and powerful (II Kings 18:23, 24; cf. I Kings 20:10). The point was undeniable, except that a gigantic army would presumably require just as much time to conquer a well-fortified city like Jerusalem as a moderate-sized army, and a lengthy siege was probably the last thing the Assyrians wanted to engage in at this time.

The most astonishing argument of all was probably the *fourth* one: "Am I now come up without Jehovah against this place to destroy it? Jehovah said unto me, Go up against this land, and destroy it" (II Kings 18:25). Nearly two centuries later, Cyrus of Persia claimed that Marduk, the god of Babylon, had "ordered him to march against his city Babylon."[3] But was this a mere propaganda technique? Isaiah had been warning Jerusalem for over thirty years that Jehovah would bring "the king of Assyria" to cause desolation in the land (Isa. 7:7-25; 8:7, 8). Jehovah's words through His prophet must have electrified the complacent Jews: "Ho Assyrian, the rod of mine anger, the staff in whose hand is mine indignation! I will send him against a profane nation, and against the people of my wrath will I give him a charge, to take the spoil, and to take the prey, and to tread them down like the mire of the streets" (Isa. 10:5, 6).

In view of the obvious cleverness of Rabshakeh, is it not possible that he had heard of Isaiah's sermons and determined to use them to his own political advantage? It seems clear that the Babylonian king was aware of Jeremiah's ministry and rewarded him accordingly after the fall of Jerusalem (Jer. 39:11, 12); and the Medo-Persians presumably knew of Daniel's denunciation of Belshazzar before the fall of Babylon (Dan. 5:28; 6:3). There is one remarkable case of a foreign king who was told by Jehovah to kill a godly king of Judah if he blocked his way through Palestine (II Chron. 35:20-22). But we may be sure that this was not true of Sennacherib, "for he hath said, By the strength of my hand I have done it, and by my wisdom" (Isa. 10:13; cf. 10:7). Furthermore, God revealed to Hezekiah that these words from the lips of the Assyrian were *blasphemies* (II Kings 19:6, 22). Even if Rabshakeh did quote from Isaiah's sermons, he failed to consider the possibility that Jehovah's wrath upon Judah would be averted if the people repented of their sins and prayed to their God.

Rabshakeh's *fifth argument* (II Kings 18:31, 32) must go down in history as one of the clumsiest and most transparent propaganda appeals on record. If you will just surrender unconditionally to us, said the Assyrian, we will provide for you free transportation to a beautiful land far away, where each of you will have a private cistern surrounded with vines, grain, and both olive and fig trees — like the Garden of Eden! The only problem with this impressive travel and settlement plan was that the sponsors had a very bad reputation! The Assyrians were

---

[3]*ANET*, p. 315.

experts in handling mass deportations from one end of the Fertile Crescent to the other, and heartless cruelty was their trademark (cf. Nah. 3:1-4, 19). Was Rabshakeh incapable of recognizing that the Judeans had a clear memory of what had happened to their northern neighbors just two decades earlier — at the hands of gentle and gracious Assyrians? (cf. II Kings 17:23, 24).

Sixth, and finally, another religious argument (II Kings 18:33-35). (In our day of near-total secularism, it is difficult to appreciate how great a role religion played in the ancient Near East, even in military and political affairs.) Other gods, that had protected greater cities than Jerusalem (the gods of Hamath, Arpad, Shepharvaim, Hena, Ivvah, and even — how pitiful! — Samaria), had proven to be utterly ineffective against the might of Ashur, god of the Assyrians. So what could Jehovah do except to surrender His city to prevent its destruction? This argument, like the second one (II Kings 18:22), must have seemed quite unimpressive to those Jews who had any concept whatsoever of the absolute uniqueness of Jehovah.

The arguments were now ended. Could they be answered and refuted on a human level? No. What, then, could they say to Rabshakeh? Nothing. "Foolish and ignorant questionings refuse, knowing that they gender strifes. And the Lord's servant must not strive . . ." (II Tim. 2:23, 24). Hezekiah did the right thing in commanding his delegation: "Answer him not" (II Kings 18:36); for the only answer the Assyrians could possibly understand would be the language of action in the form of supernatural judgment.

Hezekiah's First Prayer and God's Answer (II Kings 19:1-7)

Having been thoroughly chastened by his experience with the Assyrians, Hezekiah now set the pattern for his people in following God's way of dealing with a great crisis: (1) self-humiliation — 19:1a; (2) going to the appointed place of worship — 19:1b; (3) consulting the Word of God through His prophets — 19:2; and (4) putting God's honor and glory above everything else — 19:4. If the thrice-holy God of Israel had honored the sincere repentance of a wicked king like Ahab (I Kings 21:29), and later honored the repentant prayer of another wicked king

named Manasseh (II Chron. 33:12, 13), He would surely respond
to this kind of a prayer from this kind of a king. And Hezekiah
was not disappointed. The Lord promised through Isaiah that
the blasphemies of Rabshakeh would be dealt with. With regard to Sennacherib, God would maneuver him back to Nineveh
(possibly by a report of potential rebellion there) and cause him
to be killed at the hand of assassins (see comments on II Kings
19:37).

The Second Assyrian Threat (II Kings 19:8-13)

The words "returned" and "heard" in verses 8 and 9 are not
the fulfillments of Isaiah's prophecy (II Kings 19:7) that the king
of Assyria would "hear" and "return." Instead, verses 8 and 9
refer to a temporary shift of strategy in southern Palestine in the
light of a new threat from Tirhakah king of Ethiopia (who had
apparently usurped control of Egypt). Realizing that his position
was now more dangerous than ever, Sennacherib sent his messengers back to Jerusalem to pressure the inhabitants to surrender without a siege. Nothing new was added to previous arguments except the gruesome example of several other great cities
that had refused to surrender to the mighty Assyrian army —
Gozan, Haran, Reseph, and Telassar (II Kings 19:12; cf. 18:34).
Even as Rahab admitted to the spies that the recent reports of
Jehovah's destruction of Sihon and Og caused all of their hearts
to melt in fear (Josh. 2:10, 11), so now the example of recent
history must surely strike its mark in timid hearts.

Hezekiah's Second Prayer and God's Answer (II Kings 19:14-34)

The king's response to this fresh challenge is one of the most
encouraging examples of child-like trust in the entire Bible: "And
Hezekiah received the letter . . . and read it . . . and spread it
before Jehovah" (II Kings 19:14). How many of the discouraging
things of life do we "spread before Jehovah"? Not that He
doesn't already know all about it; but He commands us to cast
all our cares upon Him, for He cares for us (I Peter 5:7).

Hezekiah's prayer was effectual, because he knew his God and
he knew the issues in the light of God's Word: (1) Jehovah is
absolutely unique as the sovereign Creator — II Kings 19:15;

(2) a mere sinful man named Sennacherib had defied Him —
II Kings 19:16; (3) Sennacherib's boast that other gods had been
destroyed only confirmed the fact that they were not real gods
in the first place! — II Kings 19:17, 18; (4) may Jehovah be glorified among all nations by the deliverance of Jerusalem — II Kings
19:19.

God's answer to this humble and discerning prayer involved
three distinct ideas: (1) Sennacherib is a mere instrument in the
hands of a sovereign God — II Kings 19:21-28; (2) the remnant
of Israel will prosper again — II Kings 19:29-31; and (3) the Assyrians will not touch Jerusalem — II Kings 19:32-34.

First of all, Sennacherib made a fatal miscalculation when he
thought that Jerusalem was just another city (II Kings 19:21,
22)! Other great cities may have their kings (cf. Isa. 7:8, 9); but
Jerusalem also has a heavenly King who happens to be the Sovereign God of the entire earth! With insufferable pride, Sennacherib's army had destroyed one kingdom after another, like an irresponsible lumber company slashing down a beautiful forest (II
Kings 19:23). But the truth of the matter was that Jehovah had
long since planned and prepared the Assyrians for this very task
of destroying many cities (II Kings 19:25). The fact that they
couldn't resist him did not so much reflect Sennacherib's skill as
it did the irresistible purpose of Jehovah (II Kings 19:26), for
the Assyrian king was nothing but an axe, a saw, a rod, or a staff
in the hand of God (Isa. 10:15). To prove this, He would take
the raging, arrogant Assyrian by his nose and lips[4] and lead him
back to Nineveh (II Kings 19:28). What a comfort to God's
people today to know that He has "a hook in the nose" of their
arch-enemy, Satan, who can do *nothing* outside of the will of their
heavenly Father (Job 1:12; 2:5; Rev. 20:2).

Secondly, there was hope for the remnant of Judah (II Kings
19:29-31). The fruitful fields and vineyards which the Assyrians
had devastated (cf. Isa. 7:18-25) would be resown and replanted,
and by the third year the normal agricultural cycle would func-

---

[4]This was a cruelty which the Assyrians frequently inflicted upon their
captives. "Esarhaddon's relief at Zenjirli shows Tirhakah of Egypt and
Baalu of Tyre each with a ring in his nose and the cords in the hand of
the conqueror. Cf. II Chron. 33:11" (*The New Bible Commentary: Revised*), p. 363.

17. Relief of Esarhaddon, king of Assyria, from Zenjirli. Two royal captives are secured by ropes and rings through their lower lips.

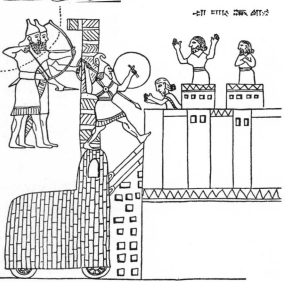

18. Assyrian mobile battering ram. It was to accommodate such a machine that Sennacherib would have built a ramp, or "cast a bank against" the wall of Jerusalem (2 Kings 19:32). Note the falling bricks loosened by the ram and the distressed defenders of the city. Courtesy, Inter-Varsity Fellowship.

tion again. To encourage his people, it is quite possible that Hezekiah wrote Psalm 126. The first three verses of this psalm reflect the national and international astonishment that Jerusalem could be delivered so suddenly from such a peril (cf. II Chron. 32:22, 23). Verse 4 is a prayer for the return of prosperity. And verses 5 and 6 are an encouragement to the remnant of Judah to sow their precious seed (instead of eating it), for even though it might involve weeping and tears, yet great joy would come with the harvesting of sheaves.

Finally, the threatened siege of Jerusalem would not materialize at all, for Jehovah would defend it to vindicate His glory which had been blasphemed (cf. I Kings 20:28), and to honor the covenant promise He had made to David (II Sam. 7). The completeness of God's protection (no arrows, shields, or mounds) reminds us of the three friends of Daniel who emerged from the fiery furnace with no clothing burned, nor hair singed, nor even the smell of fire (Dan. 3:27)! There would be no question as to who had saved Jerusalem!

The Assyrians Destroyed (II Kings 19:35-37)

That very night (compare the death of the firstborn of Egypt — Exod. 12:29) the angel of the Lord (the pre-incarnate Christ) killed 185,000 Assyrian soldiers! Is this difficult for us to believe? In order to make the narrative more palatable to the "modern mind," some have pointed to a tradition recorded by the ancient Greek historian Herodotus (ii, 141) that mice once infested a camp of the Assyrian army and ate the bow-strings and leather shield handles. The actual truth of the tradition, we are told, is the presence of mice, which would have spread bubonic plague and thus destroy the army. But would this many men die from such a cause in one night? It is also suggested that 185,000 is an exaggerated figure which somehow got into the text of II Kings. Note, for example, this unfortunate and irresponsible comment by an evangelical scholar: "there is no evidence outside of the Bible of such tremendous loss; in Chronicles it is much more moderate . . . a pestilence such as bubonic plague may have been behind both stories [i.e., Herodotus and II Kings]" (*New Bible Commentary: Revised*, Eerdmans, 1970, p. 363). Does every miracle

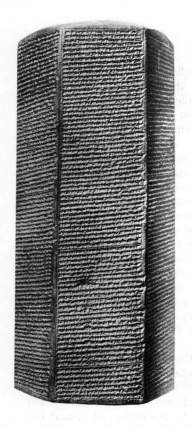

19. Hexagonal clay prism inscribed with the annals of Sennacherib, king of Assyria. Sennacherib boasts of conquering 46 strong cities of Judah and besieging Jerusalem. Courtesy, Oriental Institute.

ḫa - za - qi - a - ú   mat ia - ú - da - a - a
Hezekiah   the Judaean

kima iṣṣuri   qu - up - pi   ki - rib   al   ur - sa - li - im - mu
like a   caged bird   within   the   city of   Jerusalem

al   sami - ti - šú e - sir - šú
his   capital city   I   shut   up

20. Part of inscription appearing on Sennacherib's Prism. Courtesy, Inter-Varsity Fellowship.

recorded in the Bible have to be confirmed by outside sources before we can really believe it? Does the fact that II Chronicles 32:31 omits the number of soldiers killed contradict the number given in II Kings, *which is found also in Isaiah 37:36?* "Ye do err, not knowing the scriptures, nor the power of God" (Matt. 22:29).

However, those who are skilled at "reading between the lines" of Assyrian historical records find convincing evidence of a great Assyrian military debacle in Palestine at this time. In his famous Prism Inscription (see Fig. 19), Sennacherib states: "Hezekiah himself, whom the terror-inspiring splendor of my lordship had overwhelmed and whose irregular and elite troops which he had brought into Jerusalem, his royal residence, in order to strengthen it, had deserted him, did send me, later, to Nineveh, my lordly city, together with 30 talents of gold, 800 talents of silver. . . ."[5] Now the fact that Sennacherib said nothing about conquering Jerusalem is tantamount to admitting a total defeat, for otherwise he would have gloated over the conquest in great detail. Furthermore, it was thirteen years before the Assyrians appeared in Palestine again.

Apparently it was shortly before the destruction of his army that Sennacherib returned to his capital city of Nineveh (cf. II Kings 19:7). Twenty years later (681 B.C.), as he was worshipping in his palace chapel, two of his sons (cf. Isa. 37:38) assassinated him and fled northward to the region of Ararat between the Black Sea and the Caspian Sea. Another son, Esarhaddon (681-669 B.C.), took the throne and completed the task of transplanting Israelites to the eastern parts of the empire and replacing them with other peoples (II Kings 17:24-41; cf. Isa. 7:8; Ezra 4:2).

In a fascinating inscription, Esarhaddon tells how his father Sennacherib preferred him above his older brothers, who thereupon "abandoned godliness, put their trust in bold actions, planning an evil plot."[6] Furthermore, Ashurbanipal, the son of Esarhaddon, gives us a hint as to how Sennacherib died: ". . . others, I smashed alive with the very same statues of protective deities

---

[5]*ANET.,* p. 288.
[6]*Ibid.,* p. 289.

with which they had smashed my own grandfather Sennacherib — now finally as a belated burial sacrifice for his soul."[7]

Fitting these scraps of information together, we may assume that it was in revenge for being passed over as heirs to the throne that Esarhaddon's older brothers crept into their father's private prayer chapel and pushed over on him a gigantic statue of Nisroch, his god. And thus the great and proud king of Assyria, who boasted that Hezekiah's God was utterly helpless, not only lost his army at one flick of Jehovah's finger but was himself crushed to death by the idol of a non-existent deity to whom he had devoted his life.

[7]*Ibid.*, p. 288.

Chapter 11

HEZEKIAH AND THE BABYLONIANS

Hezekiah's Sickness (II Kings 20:1-3)

There are several reasons for believing that Hezekiah's sickness and recovery, and the visit of the ambassadors from Babylon, took place *before* the attack by Sennacherib as recorded in the previous two chapters. In the *first* place, when God responded to Hezekiah's prayer and promised to heal him, He also promised: "I will deliver thee and this city out of the hand of the king of Assyria; and I will defend this city for mine own sake, and for my servant David's sake" (II Kings 20:6). Such a promise would seem unnecessary if the Assyrian army had just been destroyed and Sennacherib had returned to Nineveh.

Secondly, it would seem highly unlikely that Hezekiah could show the Babylonian ambassadors "all the house of his precious things, the silver, and the gold . . ." (II Kings 20:13), if he had just stripped both the temple and the palace of all its gold and silver (including the plating on the doors and pillars) to buy off the Assyrians (II Kings 18:15, 16). *Thirdly,* II Chronicles 32: 25, 26 informs us that after God healed him, "Hezekiah rendered not again according to the benefit done unto him; for his heart was lifted up: therefore there was wrath upon him, and upon Judah and Jerusalem. Notwithstanding Hezekiah humbled himself for the pride of his heart, both he and the inhabitants of Jerusalem, so that the wrath of Jehovah came not upon them in the days of Hezekiah." It seems quite clear from this statement that the payment of heavy tribute and the threat of siege by Rabshakeh came *after* Hezekiah was healed of a deadly disease.

Why did the Lord tell Hezekiah to prepare to die? It is true, of course, that "it is appointed unto men once to die" (Heb. 9:27), but this is the only recorded instance of God telling a righteous man to prepare to die while he was still in the prime of life ("in the noontide of my days" — Isa. 38:10). The answer seems to be that God chose to use this means to chasten Hezekiah because of a growing pride of heart. The record in II Chronicles 29–31 of unparalleled blessings that were his during the early

125

years of revival and reformation is followed immediately by this ominous statement: "After these things, and this faithfulness, Sennacherib king of Assyria came, and entered into Judah . . ." (II Chron. 32:1). It is important to note that even *after* God healed him, "Hezekiah rendered not again according to the benefit done unto him; for his heart was lifted up . . ." (II Chron. 32:25).

The God who understands our thoughts afar off (Ps. 139:2) is jealous of our love and devotion to Him, and "whom the Lord loveth he chasteneth" (Heb. 12:6). "But I have this against thee, that thou didst leave thy first love. Remember therefore whence thou art fallen, and repent . . . or else I come to thee, and will remove thy candlestick . . ." (Rev. 2:4, 5). Only in the light of such warnings can we understand the apparent severity of God's dealings with the sins of Moses (Num. 20:12), David (II Sam. 12:10-14), and Uzziah (II Chron. 26:16-21). We may assume, then, that if II Kings 20:1 were expanded, it would read: "In those days was Hezekiah sick unto death because Jehovah chastened him for the pride that was rising within his heart after so many years of prosperity and blessing."

Just as King David "fasted and wept" when the Lord brought a great sickness upon his and Bathsheba's child (II Sam. 12:16, 22), so now "Hezekiah wept sore" under the chastening hand of a gracious God who desires nothing but the best for His children (cf. Rom. 8:28, 32). It was not that Hezekiah's years of God-honoring service had been forgotten (cf. Heb. 6:10). It was not that he had borne no spiritual fruit at all. The fact of the matter is, that *only* those who bear fruit are chastened! "Every branch that beareth fruit, he cleanseth it, that it may bear more fruit" (John 15:2). May it never be forgotten that it was Hezekiah's repentant tears, rather than his great works, that brought the *miracle* of physical healing (II Kings 20:7), the *miracle* of Jerusalem's defense (II Kings 20:6), and the *miracle* of the retreating shadow (II Kings 20:8-11).

The Promise of Recovery (II Kings 20:4-7)

One of the more unpleasant tasks God imposed upon His prophets in those days was that of pronouncing judgment upon

kings that had stepped outside of the will of God. Isaiah had
already had very unpleasant experiences with Ahaz (Isa. 7:13),
and it must have brought him great joy to see and to participate
in Hezekiah's national reforms. Nothing could have been farther
from his heart than to see now the untimely death of this great
king. We can imagine his joy, therefore, when the Lord stopped
him soon after he had given to Hezekiah the divine death sen-
tence and told him to return to the king with the assurance
that he would recover within three days and that fifteen years
would be added to his life!

What would I do with the remainder of my life if God told
me that I had just fifteen years to live? What did Hezekiah
do with those years? The Bible does not say, for the last event
recorded of his reign was the destruction of Sennacherib's army
in 701 B.C. (which probably occurred less than a year after his
sickness). It has been suggested that one reason why God prolonged his life was that he had no male heir to the throne (II
Kings 21:1 states that Manasseh was only twelve when he began
to reign). However, it is probable that Manasseh was a co-regent with his father for nearly ten years; because otherwise it
would be impossible to fit the fifty-five years of his reign into
this period of Judah's history, working back from the fixed dates
of the Babylonian Captivity (see chronology chart, p. 144) Judging from Manasseh's character (II Kings 21:1-18), Hezekiah's remaining years were not fruitful in passing on to his son the great
truths God had taught him, though his godly influence must
have been one factor in Manasseh's later deep repentance (II
Chron. 33:12, 13).

The Shadow That Returned (II Kings 20:8-11)

The statement that Hezekiah recovered (II Kings 20:7) obviously follows the giving of the sign that he would recover
(II Kings 20:8-11). For the sake of clarity, therefore, verse 8
should be translated: "And Hezekiah *had* said unto Isaiah, What
shall be the sign that Jehovah will heal me . . . ?"

It is instructive to contrast this request for a sign with the attitude of Ahaz, his father, who *refused* to ask for a faith-strength-
ening sign when the Lord promised to perform a spectacular

miracle for him "either in the depth, or in the height above"
(Isa. 7:11). Ahaz had already determined his course of action
against Pekah and Rezin, namely, to call the Assyrians to his assistance; and he was not interested in committing himself to
God's way as presented by Isaiah the prophet. Therefore his
response ("I will not ask, neither will I tempt Jehovah" — Isa.
7:12) was pure unbelief cloaked in a garment of piety. As in the
case of Moses, Gideon, Nathanael, and others, a sign could be of
great help *only* if there was genuine faith already present.

The sign that God gave to Hezekiah was certainly one of the
most spectacular miracles in Old Testament history. In the courtyard of the palace there was apparently a series of steps (not
necessarily a sundial as we would think of it) so arranged that
the shadow cast by the sun would give an approximation of
the time. At the request of the king, and doubtless in the presence of a large group of officials (including foreign ambassadors?), the shadow moved *backward* ten steps (or "degrees")!

How did God actually accomplish this miracle? Did He cause
the earth to stop its rotation and turn backwards a little? All
true Christians would agree that He *could* have done such a
thing, for by Him *all things* consist, or hold together (Col. 1:17).
But the Bible makes it rather clear that this was *not* God's
method; for in referring to this miracle, II Chronicles 32:24 states
that Hezekiah "prayed unto Jehovah; and he spake unto him,
and gave him a sign [Hebrew: *mopheth*]." But in verse 31 we
are told that the Babylonians sent ambassadors to Hezekiah "to
inquire of the wonder (*mopheth*) that was done *in the land.*"
Obviously, then, it was a *geographically localized miracle,* which
did not involve a reversal of the earth's rotation, with shadows
retreating ten degrees all over the Near East. Instead, the miracle occurred only "in the land" (of Judea); and, to be even more
specific, it was only in the king's courtyard that "the sun returned
ten steps on the dial whereon it was gone down" (Isa. 38:8).

It is the writer's conviction that a proper understanding of the
nature of this great miracle helps us to understand what happened in the miracle of Joshua's long day (Josh. 10:12-14).[1]

---

[1]See J. C. Whitcomb, "Joshua's Long Day," *Brethren Missionary Herald*
(July 27, 1963).

Since Joshua's need was a *prolongation of light* (not a slowing down of the earth's rotation), his need could be met by a supernatural continuation of sunlight and moonlight *in central Palestine* for "about a whole day" until Joshua's army could follow up its great victory and completely destroy the enemy.

The Bible teaches us that God does not unnecessarily multiply miracles. For example, Jesus did raise Lazarus, but He didn't remove the stone or the graveclothes. Furthermore, when the Flood ended, God promised to Noah that "while the earth remaineth . . . day and night shall not cease" (Gen. 8:22). This was confirmed to Jeremiah less than a century after the miracle in Hezekiah's courtyard: "If my covenant of day and night stand not . . . then will I also cast away the seed of Jacob . . ." (Jer. 33:25; cf. 31:36; 33:19). In other words, God has promised that the earth would *not* cease rotating on its axis at the present rate until the very end of human history. Vague reports of a so-called "missing day in astronomy" must therefore be investigated with extreme caution.

Hezekiah's Healing and Song of Thanksgiving (Isa. 38:9-20)

With his faith confirmed by the sign of the retreating shadow, Hezekiah gladly submitted to a fig poultice treatment on his deadly boil. The "cake of figs" did not heal him, but was a physical token of the work that God was doing, even as Jesus on one occasion put wet clay on the eyes of a blind man while healing him (John 9:6).

Isaiah's account of this miracle of healing (from which the authors of Kings and Chronicles apparently selected their materials — II Chron. 32:32) includes the song of thanksgiving which he wrote "when he had been sick and was recovered of his sickness" (Isa. 38:9). The beauty, depth, and pathos of this song demonstrates that Hezekiah was fully capable, under the direction of the Holy Spirit, of contributing significant portions to the poetical books of the Old Testament. That this song was to be used in public worship in the Temple is clearly stated in verse 20: "We will sing my songs with stringed instruments all the days of our life in the house of Jehovah."

What happened to the other songs mentioned in verse 20?

Some scholars (Lightfoot, Thirtle, Scroggie) believe that they are the ten anonymous "Songs of Degrees" in the group of fifteen (Pss. 120-134). These psalms do have a certain similarity of style, and we have already seen that Hezekiah probably composed Psalm 126 (see p. 121). It has even been suggested that Hezekiah wrote the ten anonymous psalms of this group in memory of the ten steps the shadow returned, and then added five appropriate hitherto unpublished psalms from the pens of David and Solomon (compare Prov. 25:1) to bring the total to fifteen, in honor of the fifteen years God added to his life!

The Ambassadors from Babylon (II Kings 20:12-15)

Merodach-baladan (Isa. 39:1; misspelled "Berodach" in II Kings) was twice king in Babylon, first from 722 to 710 B.C., when he was dethroned by Sargon II, and then again after Sargon died, from about 703 to 702 B.C., when Sennacherib defeated him again. The Jewish historian Josephus[2] suggests that Merodach sent his representatives to Jerusalem to gain an ally and to stir up additional trouble for the hated Assyrians. This seems highly probable as one of his motives, though the Bible only indicates two (less sinister) purposes: (1) to congratulate Hezekiah for his recovery — Isaiah and II Kings; and (2) "to inquire of the wonder (sign) that was done in the land" — II Chronicles.

The Babylonians were indeed fascinated by astronomic signs, for their national life revolved around the movement of planets and comets against the background of fixed stars and the predicted time intervals of solar and lunar eclipses. Expert "stargazers" (called "soothsayers" in Dan. 2:27) spent their lives taking amazingly accurate astronomic measurements in order to control the superstitious population through astrology. Isaiah challenged these men to save Babylon from divine judgment if they could: "let now the astrologers, the star-gazers, the monthly prognosticators, stand up, and save thee from the things that shall come upon thee" (Isa. 47:13). Because of these Babylonian astrologers, millions of heathen were "dismayed at the signs of

---

[2]*Ant.* x.2.2.

heaven" (Jer. 10:2), and we must admit with sorrow that their influence is gaining momentum even in so-called Christian America today.[3]

Thus, the Babylonians were particularly amazed and alarmed to hear about the return of the sun's shadow at the word of King Hezekiah of Judah, and they were convinced that he had some secret powers for manipulating the heavenly bodies. Perhaps a man such as this could be persuaded or bribed into accomplishing the destruction of Assyria by controlling the celestial signs!

Hezekiah was "glad" to see these ambassadors (Isa. 39:2), and thus failed an important spiritual test; for God allowed this to happen "to try him, that he might know all that was in his heart" (II Chron. 32:31). What did the test reveal — a deep suspicion of the motives of these pagans? An abiding concern for the glory of the God who had healed him and spared his life? No, his heart's desire was to convince these men that he was not a second-rate king according to the world's standards. And so, instead of learning about the uniqueness and holiness of Jehovah, and the necessity of acknowledging him alone, they carried back to Babylon nothing more than a knowledge of silver, gold, spices, precious oil, and material treasures (II Kings 20:13). Thus, "Hezekiah rendered not again according to the benefit done unto him; for his heart was lifted up" (II Chron. 32:25).

Coming Judgment (II Kings 20:16-19)

The judgment that came upon Hezekiah and his people (who obviously shared his attitude of sinful pride and complacency) was twofold. *First,* within a matter of months the Assyrians would threaten Jerusalem with destruction, and it would be only by a timely repentance on the part of both king and people that the city would be spared ("therefore there was wrath upon him and upon Judah and Jerusalem. Notwithstanding Hezekiah humbled himself for the pride of his heart, both he and the inhabitants of Jerusalem, so that the wrath of Jehovah came not upon them in the days of Hezekiah" — II Chron. 32:25, 26).

Second, the very Babylonians in whom he had delighted would

---

[3]*Time,* March 21, 1969.

some day strip his palace of everything (just as the Assyrians would do within a few months), carry his descendants into captivity, and make some of them serve as eunuchs in the palace of Babylon (II Kings 20:17, 18; this probably does not refer to Daniel and his three friends "in whom was no blemish" — Dan. 1:4). Instead of collapsing before the Lord in deep repentance, Hezekiah's response (in the spirit of Neville Chamberlain after Munich in 1939) was incredibly and criminally shallow: "Good is the word of Jehovah which thou hast spoken. . . . Is it not so, if peace and truth shall be in my days?" (II Kings 20:19). Harold Stigers comments: "This was not a confession of sin. It was an expression of the 'peace in our time' policy, that short-sighted attitude that shows little concern for those on whom coming catastrophe shall fall. Therefore Isaiah could only turn to Jehovah and cry out, 'Comfort ye, comfort ye my people' (Isa. 40:1). Only after the predicted destruction would there come an end to Israel's sin of apostasy, and only then would true peace endure."[4]

---

[4]*Wycliffe Bible Commentary* (Moody Press, 1962), p. 362.

Chapter 12

JOSIAH'S REFORMATION

Manasseh and Amon (II Kings 21:1-26)

In spite of the probability that Manasseh became king (or co-regent) about ten years before Hezekiah died, the godly influence of his father created only a negative reaction in the heart of this delinquent teen-ager. Shocking as this record of royal depravity may be, especially following the great revival of true religion in Hezekiah's day, we have ample illustrations from our own times of just such reversals. Cultured, and even godly, homes are no *guarantee* of high quality among children, because each child begins at zero, spiritually speaking (Ps. 51:5; 58:3). God may have children (according to the riches of His grace), but not grandchildren! Compare Ezekiel's analysis of the righteous father, the wicked son, and the righteous grandson (18: 5-18) with Hezekiah, Manasseh (and Amon), and Josiah.

For half a century, Manasseh deliberately duplicated the depravity of the Canaanites whom Joshua was commissioned to destroy (II Kings 21:9; cf. II Chron. 33:9). In fact, he murdered so many righteous men in Jerusalem that the remnant became too small to spare the nation from total destruction, in spite of the noble reforming efforts of Josiah (II Kings 21:10-15; cf. 23:26). The fact that the majority of the people tolerated the utter paganism of Manasseh was God's reason for sealing the doom of the city and the Temple, and there could be no escape. God even told Jeremiah: "Pray not thou for this people . . . for I will not hear thee" (Jer. 7:16; cf. 11:14; 14:11). Their hearts had been judicially hardened (cf. Isa. 6:9-12).

Included in the "innocent blood" that Manasseh shed (II Kings 21:16) may have been that of the prophet Isaiah himself; for Jewish tradition relates that he was "sawn asunder" (cf. Heb. 11:37).[1] Is it possible for a man as wicked as Manasseh to turn

---

[1]Whatever Manasseh may have done to Isaiah in the seventh century B.C., negative critics of the nineteenth century A.D. busied themselves in cutting Isaiah's book asunder, with "Deutero-" and other "Isaiahs" to explain away the magnificent predictive prophecies God gave to Israel through his pen (e.g., Isa. 44:28; 45:1).

133

to God in genuine repentance? Ezekiel said it was possible (18:21-24, 27, 28), and II Chronicles 33:13 tells us that he did! For some offense against Ashurbanipal, the king of Assyria, Manasseh was dragged to Babylon "with hooks" (ASV margin; cf. II Kings 19:28). While in prison, "he besought Jehovah his God, and humbled himself greatly before the God of his fathers. And he prayed unto him; and he was entreated of him, and heard his supplication, and brought him again to Jerusalem into his king-

21. King Ashurbanipal shooting from saddle with bow and arrow. Relief fom Nineveh, c. 650 B.C. Courtesy, Inter-Varsity Fellowship.

dom. Then Manasseh knew that Jehovah, he was God" (II Chron. 33:12). Just as Joseph's brethren, while in prison, remembered his desperate entreaties, their consciences being activated by extreme adversity (Gen. 42:21); so now Manasseh must have recalled the teachings of his godly father and the warnings of the prophets whom he had slain (II Chron. 33:10).

How much of his 55-year reign was left after this we have no way of knowing; but it was now too late to reverse the trends he had initiated. His wicked son Amon cancelled these belated reforms and soon died at the hands of assassins.

Josiah's Initial Reforms (II Kings 22:1-7; II Chron. 34:1-13)

The author of II Chronicles lists for us in loving detail the chronological progress of Josiah's great reformation movement. Who it was in such a corrupt society that instructed and challenged him (apart from the Spirit of God) we are not told. At the tender age of *eight* he began to reign (II Chron. 34:1). At the age of *sixteen* "he began to seek after the God of David his father" (II Chron. 34:3). At about the same time, Ashurbanipal, king of Assyria, died and the once-mighty empire began to fall apart. At the age of *twenty* Josiah began to cleanse the land of all the tokens and instruments of idolatry (II Chron. 34:3-7). A year later the prophet Jeremiah began his ministry (Jer. 25:3). At the age of *twenty-six* Josiah began to repair the Temple with money collected from the remnant of *all* the tribes, delivering it to Hilkiah the high priest (34:8, 9).

Finding the Book of the Law (II Kings 22:8-13)

In the process of cleansing the Temple of the heaps of rubbish that had accummulated during the reigns of Manasseh and Amon, the high priest Hilkiah discovered a copy of "the book of the law" (II Kings 22:8). Hilkiah gave it to Shaphan the scribe to read, who in turn came to the king. Mentioning first that the Temple repairs were proceeding according to schedule, Shaphan then dropped a delayed-fuse bomb with enormous disruptive power — Jehovah's despised and neglected warnings of national judgment! King Josiah was utterly overwhelmed when he heard God's description of apostasy and its consequences echoing through the centuries from the time of Moses, and he feared that it might already be too late to bring the nation to repentance.

What was "the book of the law" that Hilkiah discovered? Some Bible students believe that it was the entire Pentateuch, while others claim that it was either the Book of Deuteronomy or just certain sections like Leviticus 26 and Deuteronomy 28 which enumerate the judgments God would bring upon His people if they continued to defy His Word. It is frankly quite difficult to imagine that a Davidic king could be unaware of such a significant portion of Scripture, especially when God had so clearly commanded that each king must "write him a copy of this law in a book, out of that which is before the priests and Levites: and it shall be with him, and he shall read therein all the days of his life" (Deut. 17:18). Did not even the priests and Levites have copies of the Law, which it was their special responsibility to teach to the people? (cf. Lev. 10:11, II Chron. 17:9; 35:3; Neh. 8:7; Mal. 2:6, 7).

In seeking to answer this important question, we must remember that Manasseh had wiped out almost every trace of the true religion of Israel during a period of fifty years. As in the later persecutions of the Jews by Antiochus Epiphanes (168 B.C.) and of the Christians by the Roman emperor Diocletian (*ca.* A.D. 290), so also in Manasseh's persecution of Israel's godly remnant, it was probably a capital offense to possess a copy of the Scriptures. Thus, whatever copies of the sacred scrolls actually survived this period were probably hidden in caves like those near the Dead Sea where so many priceless manuscripts have been discovered.

In passing, we must comment on one of the most fantastic fables ever foisted upon the Church by "the father of lies." Nineteenth century A.D. negative critics of the Old Testament, especially a German scholar named Julius Wellhausen, insisted that the book of Deuteronomy was invented by an unknown contemporary of King Josiah. Making the scroll to read like an original production of Moses himself, he planted it in the rubbish heaps of the Temple in order that it might be discovered during the time of cleansing and repair! The true tragedy of this fantastic theory is that the vast majority of Old Testament scholars in Europe and America adopted it, and its influence continues to the present hour, even though the theory has experienced many modifications (see *The New Bible Commentary: Revised,* 1970, pp. 34-40).

Huldah's Prophecy (II Kings 22:14-20)

The king immediately requested that Jehovah be consulted through His appointed prophets concerning these fearsome words of divine warning. Was there yet hope for the nation? Five years before this, Jeremiah had begun his prophetic ministry in Judah; and Zephaniah was also proclaiming the word of the Lord. But apparently neither of these men was in Jerusalem at this time. So Josiah's official representatives went to a prophetess in Jerusalem named Huldah, who was probably an aunt of Jeremiah (II Kings 22:14; cf. Jer. 32:7).

This was not the first time that Jehovah had spoken to the nation through a woman. *Miriam,* the sister of Moses, was a prophetess (Exod. 15:20); *Deborah* led the nation in a time of crisis and composed an inspired song of victory (Judges 5); and Isaiah's wife was also called a prophetess (Isa. 8:3). In New Testament times we recall that Anna (Luke 2:36) and the four daughters of Philip the evangelist (Acts 21:9) received this special gift from God for speaking forth His infallible words of truth.

It is interesting that Huldah did not refer to Josiah as "the king" in her first reference to him, but simply as "the man" (II Kings 22:15). This was not disrespectful, but apparently was God's way of emphasizing the frailty of one who, though king, needed His help desperately. In spite of Josiah's well-meaning efforts, the reformation was essentially superficial; for almost everyone involved in this great "revival" was insincere except the king and a tiny remnant of true believers. Jeremiah seems to suggest this very problem when he said in one of his earlier sermons: "Judah hath not returned unto me with her whole heart, but feignedly, saith Jehovah" (Jer. 3:10). As has been true in all too many "revival meetings" since then, God was "near in their mouth, and far from their heart" (Jer. 12:2).

For these reasons, the judgment of God, though postponed, would be certain. Apostasy and paganism were too deeply entrenched in the hearts of the people to be rooted out by mere decrees emanating from the royal palace. But God would spare Josiah from seeing the coming national catastrophe, even as he had spared Hezekiah three generations earlier, "because thy heart was tender, and thou didst humble thyself before Jehovah, when thou heardest what I spake against this place" (II Kings 22:19).

It may seem strange indeed that God would have promised Josiah: "thou shalt be gathered to thy grave in peace" (II Kings 22:20), when, as a matter of fact, he was killed by an Egyptian pharaoh on the field of battle! (cf. II Chron. 35:23). The problem is solved, however, when we realize that for the Israelite, to die "in peace" meant to die in a state of fellowship with God as a true believer, whether in the front line of battle or at home in bed. In contrast to this, "there is no peace, saith my God, to the wicked" (Isa. 57:21).

The Covenant Renewed and Reforms Intensified
(II Kings 23:1-20)

Deeply shocked by the word of God through Huldah the prophetess, King Josiah gathered the leaders of the nation to the Temple for a public reading of the newly-discovered portions of Scripture. Then he encouraged all the people to stand with him in a renewal of covenant vows to Jehovah.

As we read in the following verses some of the details of Josiah's great reform movement, we are astounded at the mass of idolatrous influences that had been allowed to accummulate in the kingdom, the capital city, and the Temple courts:

(1) The paraphernalia of paganism were carted out of the Temple and burned in the Kidron Valley, the ashes being used to defile the rival center of Israelite worship at Bethel (II Kings 23:4).

(2) The idolatrous priests (Hebrew, *Chemarim*; cf. Hos. 10: 5; Zeph. 1:4) were "put down."

(3) The Asherah (the idol of Baal's consort) was removed from the Temple and burned.

(4) The tents that male Baal-cult prostitutes ("Sodomites") had set up in the Temple courts were removed.

(5) Priests throughout Judah were recruited to defile idolatrous high places.

(6) The place of human sacrifice to Molech (god of Ammon) in the Valley of Hinnom, just south of the city, was defiled.

(7) Chariots dedicated to the use of the sun god were burned.
(8) Special heathen altars erected by Ahaz and Manasseh in the Temple courts were destroyed.
(9) Sacred shrines which Solomon had erected for his foreign wives on the surrounding hills were destroyed (cf. I Kings 11:5-8).
(10) Jeroboam's rival altar at Bethel, and all other Samaritan altars, were destroyed and desecrated with the exhumed bones of their priests (cf. I Kings 13:2).
(11) All surviving calf-worshipping priests were slain.
(12) All mediums and wizards were removed from the land (cf. II Kings 21:6).

As we ponder this amazing list, we cannot help but ask what had been accomplished during the previous six years of reforms. It will be recalled that a great national purge of idols had begun in Josiah's *twelfth* official year (II Chron. 34:3), and the present purge took place in his *eighteenth* year. We can only conclude that the task was so gigantic that it took many years to complete. Furthermore, the reform movement may have started slowly because of fear of offending the Assyrian overlords. But as the collapse of Assyrian power following the death of Ashurbanipal became evident to all, and as Jeremiah's powerful messages struck deep into the consciences of the people, the reformation began to increase in momentum.

Another important question arises: What was really accomplished by this great reformation? Were any of the fundamental spiritual problems of the people solved? Was there a widespread turning of hearts to the Lord? Was the nation now in a position to serve and glorify their God? The answer to these questions, unfortunately, is *no.* This might come as a great surprise to many in our own day who feel that their best energies should be spent on reform movements, purging the nation of this or that physical or moral evil. That such evils are ruining the nation and should be uprooted no sensible person would deny. But the problem is how to deal with the *source,* not the final product; with the *root,* not the ultimate fruit. Every true Christian is (or should be) concerned with the problems of environmental pollution, drugs, crime, pornography, governmental inefficiency, communism, war, etc., etc., which threaten the health, morals, and very existence of our society. But if the source and root of these problems is not recognized and dealt with in the light of God's Word, nothing of permanent value can be accomplished for anyone.

Our Lord told of a man (or, in our case, a nation) from which an evil spirit was expelled (Matt. 12:43). Returning, he found that there had been a great reformation — he found it "empty, swept, and garnished." "Then goeth he, and taketh with himself seven other spirits more evil than himself, and they enter in and dwell there: and the last state of that man [or nation] became worse than the first. Even so shall it be also unto this evil generation." Here is the abiding lesson of Josiah's reforms. "Out of *the heart* come forth evil thoughts, murders. . ." (Matt. 15:19; cf. 12:33-35), and unless *the heart* is dealt with by the Holy Spirit speaking through His Word, there can be neither salvation nor permanent reformation (cf. Heb. 4:12; Eph. 2:1-10; Rom. 8:1-4; Ezek. 36:26, 27).

The Great Passover (II Kings 23:21-23; cf. II Chron. 35:1-19)

Full details of Josiah's great passover celebration in 622 B.C. are provided for us in II Chronicles 35. Three points of special interest should be noted in this account. *First,* it appears that conditions had deteriorated so badly in the Temple since the days of Hezekiah that faithful Levites had removed and hidden the Ark of God! (II Chron. 35:3). Josiah ordered it to be returned, for there could be no proper observance of the passover without it. *Second,* the Levites showed extraordinary zeal in preparing passover lambs, not only for themselves, but also for the priests, the singers, and the porters (II Chron. 35:11-15; cf. Ezra 6:20). *Third,* this was the greatest passover since the days of Samuel the prophet 500 years earlier (II Chron 35:18), because of the obstacles that had to be overcome and because it was done with such great zeal and according to the Law (Hezekiah's passover had to be held on the second month because so many were ceremonially defiled — II Chron. 30:2, 3, 17-20).

The Death of Josiah (II Kings 23:28-30; II Chron. 35:20-27)

The final years of Josiah's reign saw tremendous changes taking place on the international scene. Nineveh had finally fallen under the combined attacks of Medes and Babylonians in 612 B.C., and a remnant of the Assyrian army under Ashuruballit II fled westward to a stronghold on the Euphrates River named Carchemish. By 609 B.C., the Babylonian army was preparing to cross the Euphrates to conquer Syria, having by now consolidated their newly conquered territories to the east. Desiring to block a Babylonian move into Palestine, and to gain control of Syria for themselves, the Egyptians (whose power had increased in ratio to the decline of Assyria) determined to move north to Carchemish and back the Assyrians in their desperate last-ditch stand against the Babylonians.

The statement that "Pharaoh-necho king of Egypt went up against the king of Assyria to the river Euphrates" (II Kings 23:29) should better be translated: "*on behalf of* the king of Assyria, to the river Euphrates."[2] It was at this point that Josiah made his fatal mistake. Thinking, perhaps, that any friend of the hated Assyrians was an enemy of his, and boldly disregarding all prophetic warnings against meddling in international affairs, he quickly moved his army to Megiddo to block the Egyptian army.

Now came one of the strangest episodes in Old Testament history. The heathen king, Necho II of Egypt, informed Josiah that "God hath commanded me to make haste" and that if Josiah interfered with God's plan, God would destroy him (II Chron. 35:21). We would immediately dismiss such a statement as propaganda, of course, were it not for the explanation by the Chronicler that Josiah "hearkened not unto the words of Necho *from the mouth of God*" (II Chron. 35:22)! Furthermore, Necho must be believed, for Josiah *was* killed. What does this mean? Did Josiah lose his salvation because of disobedience? No, for Huldah had said he would die "in peace" (II Chron. 34:28). Was Pharaoh-necho a prophet of Jehovah? No, for God had spoken to pagan kings directly at various times without neces-

---

[2]J. Barton Payne in *The Wycliffe Bible Commentary*, p. 419.

sarily transforming their hearts (see Gen. 12:17-20; 20:3-7). We may conclude that God wanted to maneuver the Egyptian army to the Euphrates so that Nebuchadnezzar could destroy it as well as the Assyrian army, and thus fulfill His warning that the Babylonians would conquer and chasten Judah (see Jer. 25:8-11).

Even more tragic than the fact of Josiah's death was the manner of his death. Disguising himself like Ahab (cf. I Kings 22:30), thus hoping to avoid the deadly wound that he must have suspected God was planning for him, he challenged the Egyptian army in the Valley of Megiddo, only to be pierced by an arrow that was God's key to the grave where he would be "gathered to his fathers in peace."

Great was the national mourning for Josiah. The great reformation was obviously over, for his sons offered no prospect of walking in their father's footsteps. Someday, wrote the prophet Zechariah a century later, Israel will mourn for the Messiah they crucified, even "as the mourning of Hadadrimmon in the valley of Megiddon" (12:11), a remarkable evidence of the intensity and universality of Judah's mourning for Josiah. Jeremiah lamented for Josiah too (II Chron. 35:25; these lamentations are not found in the Book of Lamentations which is concerned with the fall of Jerusalem); and to protect the uniqueness of Josiah's reputation, Jeremiah commanded the nation *not* to mourn over the exile of Shallum (or Jehoahaz — Jer. 22:10-12) or the death of Jehoiakim (Jer. 22:18). Truly, Josiah was a great and godly king; but it would take more than a Josiah to reverse the downward trend of the nation: "Though Moses and Samuel stood before me, yet my mind would not be toward this people: cast them out of my sight, and let them go forth" (Jer. 15:1). In the final chapter it will be our unpleasant responsibility to see how God did this very thing.

Chapter 13

THE BABYLONIAN CAPTIVITY

Jehoahaz/Shallum, the Exile to Egypt
(II Kings 23:30-34, II Chron. 36:1-4)

The tragic death of Josiah at Megiddo marked the end of true quality in the royal line of Judah until the return of Christ to sit "upon the throne of David . . . to establish it, and to uphold it with justice and with righteousness from henceforth even for ever" (Isa. 9:7).

As Pharaoh Necho marched his army to the Euphrates in June, 609 B.C., to help the Assyrian army block any further Babylonian advances towards the west, the people of Judah put Josiah's son Jehoahaz upon the throne in Jerusalem.[1] But his evil reign was a short one, for Pharaoh Necho deposed him at the end of the summer on his return from the Euphrates, and carried him off to Egypt, and elevated Eliakim to the throne. The prophet Jeremiah, who called him "Shallum," proclaimed an oracle against him: "He shall not return thither any more; but in the place whither they have led him captive, there shall he die, and he shall see this land no more" (Jer. 22:11-12). Little did Jeremiah realize that he himself would ultimately be dragged to Egypt in a miniature reversal of the Exodus, never to return to the land he loved (cf. Jer. 43, 44).

Jehoiakim, the Prophet Hater
(II Kings 23:34—24:7; II Chron. 36:4-8)

For some reason, Pharaoh Necho felt that Eliakim, a brother of Jehoahaz, would be a more dependable vassal. To improve Eliakim's image with the traditionalists in Judah, Necho changed his name to Jehoiakim. But this was hardly sufficient to offset

---

[1] In 609 B.C., Jehoiakim was the oldest son of Josiah at 25; Jehoahaz was 23, and Zedekiah was only 10. In I Chron. 3:15, however, Johoahaz/ Shallum is listed as the last of four sons of Josiah.

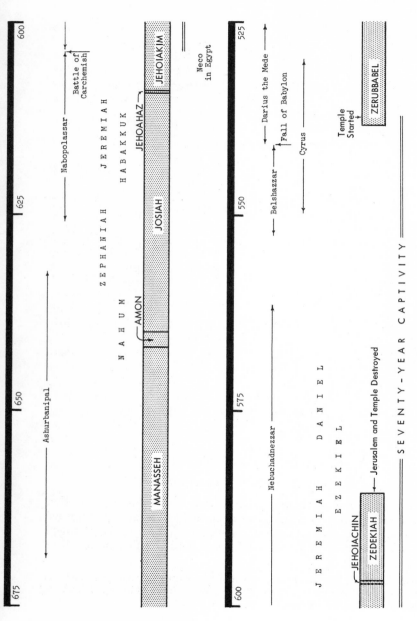

22. Time Chart: 675 to 525 B.C.

the vast unpopularity the new king must have incurred when he taxed the people heavily to pay tribute to the Egyptians (II Kings 23:35).[2] To make matters worse, while the people groaned under these burdens Jehoiakim built for himself a luxurious palace "ceiled with cedar and painted with vermillion" (Jer. 22:14) and then refused to pay the workers (Jer. 22:13).

Jehoiakim was probably the most consistently wicked king of Judah since Ahaz (cf. Jer. 22:15-17). He took a scroll of Jeremiah's sermons, calmly cut it into pieces, and threw it into the fire after hearing only three or four columns read (Jer. 36:20-26). He twice attempted to capture Jeremiah, but was thwarted through the intervention of God and friends (Jer. 26:24; 36:19, 26; cf. 1:19). However, he did kill the prophet Uriah who preached "according to all the words of Jeremiah" (Jer. 26:20-23).

In Jehoiakim's fourth year (the summer of 605 B.C.), Pharaoh Necho once again led his army to the Euphrates for a confrontation with the Babylonians. Nabopolassar, king of Babylon, was sick at home while his son Nebuchadnezzar led the army. Jeremiah had already prophesied that Nebuchadnezzar would not only win this battle but would also control Judah for seventy years (Jer. 25:1-11; cf. Hab. 1:1-17). And so the Egyptian army, led like sacrificial animals to the slaughter (Jer. 46:10), received wounds from Nebuchadnezzar that all the balm of Gilead could never heal (Jer. 46:2, 11). In a recently translated tablet, the official scribe of Babylon tells the story: "In the 21st year [605/04 B.C.] the king of Akkad stayed in his own land, Nebuchadrezzar his eldest son, the crown-prince, mustered (the Babylonian army) and took command of the troops; he marched to Carchemish which is on the bank of the Euphrates, and crossed the river (to go) against the Egyptian army which lay in Carchemish . . . fought with each other and the Egyptian army withdrew before him. He accomplished their defeat and to nonexistence (beat) them. As for the rest of the Egyptian army

---

[2]The progressive poverty of the nation may be detected in the amount of tribute that could be exacted. Hezekiah paid 300 talents of silver and 30 talents of gold (II Kings 18:14). But Jehoiachin could pay only 100 talents of silver and one talent of gold.

which escaped from the defeat (so quickly that) no weapon had reached them, in the district of Hamath the Babylonian troops overtook and defeated them so that not a single man (escaped) to his own country. At that time Nebuchadnezzar conquered the whole area of the Hatti-country (Syria, Phoenicia, and Palestine]."[3]

Sweeping into Palestine in pursuit of the Egyptians, Nebuchadnezzar's troops besieged Jerusalem until Jehoiakim surrendered.[4] The Chronicler says that Nebuchadnezzar "bound him in fetters to carry him to Babylon" (II Chron. 36:6); but before the plan was fulfilled something of urgent importance happened that caused Nebuchadnezzar to change his mind. He received word that his father Nabopolassar had died in Babylon on August 15. Realizing that the throne was now in jeopardy, he forced Jehoiakim to promise loyalty as his vassal,[5] took the short route across the Arabian desert to Babylon,[6] and sent some prisoners (including Daniel and his friends) the long way around. The Babylonian chronicle informs us that Nebuchadnezzar "sat on the royal throne in Babylon" by September 6, 605 B.C., which was only twenty-three days after his father died!

Like Hoshea, the last king of Israel, Jehoiakim must have felt the increasing pressure of the pro-Egyptian party in his kingdom. After three years of paying tribute to Nebuchadnezzar, he finally decided, against the vigorous warnings of Jeremiah (cf. Jer. 36:29), to rebel against the Babylonian monarch (II Kings 24:1). But God raised up various marauding bands from the north and east to harass Jehoiakim until he was finally killed in early December, 598 B.C. Jeremiah had predicted that "they shall not lament for him, saying, Ah lord! or, Ah his glory! He

---

[3]Donald J. Wiseman, *Chronicles of Chaldean Kings* (London: The Trustees of the British Museum, 1956), pp. 67, 69.

[4]Daniel 1:1. The "third year of the reign of Jehoiakim" in this verse is not a contradiction to "the fourth year of Jehoiakim" in Jer. 25:1, for according to Daniel's Tishri reckoning Jehoiakim's fourth official year would not begin until the fall of 605 B.C.

[5]This is implied in II Kings 24:1. Wiseman (*op. cit.*, p. 28) suggests that the three-year servitude did not begin until 604 B.C.

[6]According to the Babylonian historian Berossus, as quoted by Josephus, *Contra Apionem*, I, 19.

shall be buried with the burial of an ass, drawn and cast forth beyond the gates of Jerusalem" (Jer. 22:18-19; cf. 36:30). Furthermore, "he shall have none to sit upon the throne of David" (Jer. 36:30), which must have been an anticipation of the curse which would fall upon his son, Jehoiachin.

Jehoiachin, the Broken Vessel
(II Kings 24:8-16; II Chron. 36:9-10)

Jehoiachin's wicked reign began and ended when he was only eighteen years old, for he ruled for only three months and ten days (II Chron. 36:9).[7] Because of his father's treasonous acts, the Babylonian army besieged Jerusalem and finally captured it on March 15, 597 B.C. This date has finally come to light through the remarkably detailed Babylonian Chronicle: "the king of Akkad mustered his troops, marched to the Hatti-land, and encamped against the city of Judah and on the second day of the month Adar he seized the city and captured the king. He appointed there a king of his own choice, received its heavy tribute and sent them to Babylon."[8]

23. Judaean prisoners going into captivity to Assyria. The Babylonians followed the policy initiated by the Assyrians of deporting populations. Courtesy, Inter-Varsity Fellowship.

[7]He could hardly have been eight years old at this time, for he had wives (II Kings 24:15). Therefore the number "eight" in II Chron. 36:9 should read "eighteen" as in II Kings 24:8.

[8]Wiseman, *op. cit.*, p. 73.

Jehoiachin, together with his mother Nehushta, his wives, and ten thousand of his leading citizens came out of the city to receive their judgment from the lips of Nebuchadnezzar himself: permanent deportation to Babylon. More treasures were taken from the Temple (cf. Dan. 1:2 for the sacred vessels taken in 605 B.C.), leaving just enough sacred furniture for religious ceremonies to be carried on under the high priest Seraiah and the puppet king Zedekiah (II Kings 25:13-18).

Among the captives taken to Babylon at this time was a young priest named Ezekiel. Five years later, at the age of thirty, he began to prophesy to the exiles in Babylon, explaining why Jerusalem was doomed to destruction and why the Shekinah Glory had departed from the Temple (Ezek. 1-33). Ezekiel continued to date his own ministry in terms of Jehoiachin's reign (Ezek. 1:2), because as long as Jehoiachin lived he (*not* his uncle Zedekiah) was Judah's legitimate king. However, Jeremiah made it clear that Jehoiachin was the *last* legitimate king of Judah, "for no more shall a man of his seed prosper, sitting upon the throne of David, and ruling in Judah" (Jer. 22:30).[9]

A remarkable series of Babylonian tablets have been discovered which list foreign prisoners who received rations from the royal storehouses from 595 to 570 B.C.

> Among them Jehoiachin (Yaukin), his five sons and eight other Judeans are named together with other royalty and craftsmen from places in Egypt, Philistia (Ashkelon), Phoenicia, Syria, Cilicia, Lydia, Elam, Media and Persia, some of which are mentioned in the prophecies of Jeremiah. Jehoiachin, held as a hostage, was still called "king of Judah." His royal estates in Judah continued to be managed, at least between 597 and 587, by "Eliakim, steward of Jehoiachin," impressions of whose seal were found at Debir and Bethshemesh.[10]

---

[9]Ezekiel explained that the kingship would be removed from Judah "until he come whose right it is" (21:27); namely, Christ. See pp. 101-102 for a discussion of how God solved this apparent contradiction of perpetual kingship through Solomon (II Sam. 7) and a perpetual curse upon Solomon's descendant, Jehoiachin.

[10]Donald J. Wiseman, *Illustrations from Biblical Archaeology* (Grand Rapids: Wm. B. Eerdmans Publishing Co., 1958), p. 73.

It seems probable that toward the close of Nebuchadnezzar's reign Jehoiachin was involved in some treasonous plot; for when Nebuchadnezzar died in 562 B.C., his son Evil-merodach "did lift up the head of Jehoiachin king of Judah out of prison; and he spoke kindly to him, and set his throne above the throne of the kings that were with him in Babylon, and changed his prison garments. And Jehoiachin did eat bread before him continually all the days of his life: and for his allowance, there was a continual allowance given him of the king, every day a portion, all the days of his life" (II Kings 25:28-30). We can understand this as Evil-merodach's effort to gain favor with subject peoples, especially the Jews, who might be tempted to revolt after the death of his powerful father.

Zerubbabel, who led nearly 50,000 Jews back to Judah in 537 B.C., was a grandson of Jehoiachin (Matt. 1:12). He knew that he could never be Judah's king because of Jeremiah's curse, but God compensated with the assurance that "I will make thee as a signet, for I have chosen thee" (Hag. 2:23; contrast Jer. 22:24).

Zedekiah, the Fickle Puppet
(II Kings 24:18—25:7; II Chron. 36:10-21)

Having sent Jehoiachin to Babylon, Nebuchadnezzar placed his uncle Mattaniah on the throne, changing his name to Zedekiah ("Jehovah is righteous"!) and making him swear by Jehovah that he would remain loyal (II Chron. 36:13; Ezek. 17:11-21). It is just possible that Nebuchadnezzar refrained from destroying Jerusalem at this time because of the intervention of Daniel, who five years earlier had been established in the court of Babylon as the supreme interpreter of dreams (Dan. 2:1, 46-49). If so, he blundered seriously in not leaving Zedekiah in the hands of more qualified advisors, for the puppet king was apparently helpless to bring Judah into submission to Babylon even if he wanted to.[11] Zedekiah and the nobles who were permitted to remain in Judah convinced themselves that they were God's

---

11 F. F. Bruce, *Israel and the Nations* (Grand Rapids: Wm. B. Eerdmans Publishing Co., 1963), p. 89.

chosen ones, while the exiles were being punished for their special sins. Both Jeremiah and Ezekiel denounced this attitude,
explaining that Jehovah would henceforth treat the exiles as
"good figs" (Jer. 24) and would "be to them a sanctuary for a
little while in the countries where they are come" (Ezek. 11:
16). In fact, Jeremiah wrote a letter to the exiles stating that
Jehovah had "thoughts of peace, and not of evil, to give you
hope in your latter end" (Jer. 29:11).

In his fourth year (593 B.C.), Zedekiah had to appear before
Nebuchadnezzar in Babylon, presumably to promise again that
he would not betray his oath or look toward Egypt for help
(Jer. 51:59-64). In the same year, the Lord instructed Jeremiah
to prepare some "bonds and bars" as symbols of submission to
Nebuchadnezzar, and to present them to the ambassadors of
five western kingdoms in Jerusalem to take back to their kings.
But all to no avail. Zedekiah's vacillation between submission
to Babylon and flirtation with Egypt finally brought upon him
the wrath of Nebuchadnezzar, as well as the wrath of Jehovah
whose Name Zedekiah had uttered in his oath of loyalty (Ezek.
17:11-21).[12] Because of this, Ezekiel referred to him as the
"deadly wounded wicked one, the prince of Israel, whose day
is come . . ." (Ezek. 21:25; cf. vs. 14).

Nebuchadnezzar had long been distracted by military com-
mitments elsewhere in his vast empire and even a revolt within
his own army in 594 B.C.[13] But now he was free to bring his
iron fist down upon rebellious Judah, whose day, like that of
Zedekiah, had fully come. Using divination to decide whether
to attack Rabbah of Ammon first, Nebuchadnezzar was led by
God to move directly to Jerusalem, "to set battering rams, to
open the mouth in the slaughter, to lift up the voice with shouting . . . to cast up mounds, to build forts" (Ezek. 21:18-22).
The final agony of Judah had begun.

Because the siege began in Zedekiah's ninth year, the tenth
month, and ended in his eleventh year, the fourth month, it

---

[12]The solemnity and permanence of oaths uttered in the Name of
Jehovah are greatly emphasized in the Old Testament (cf. Num. 30:2; Ps.
50:14; 66:13-14; Eccles. 5:4).

[13] Donald J. Wiseman, *Chronicles of Chaldaean Kings,* pp. 36, 37, 73.

has generally been assumed that the siege lasted for eighteen
months (January 588 to July 587 B.C.). However, the siege
must have lasted *thirty months*, because Ezekiel states that it
began in the tenth month of Jehoiachin's *ninth* year (Ezek. 24:
1) and the word of Jerusalem's destruction reached Babylonia
in the tenth month of his *twelfth* year, exactly three years later
(Ezek. 33:21). Thus, Jerusalem fell on July 18, 586 B.C., and six
months later the tragic news came to Ezekiel in Babylon. In the
light of Ezekiel's clear chronology, it becomes obvious that the
author of Kings was using a Tishri dating system (with the
first day of the seventh month being the beginning of the king's
official year) in II Kings 25, so that the tenth month would be
early in his ninth year, and the fourth month would be *late* in
his eleventh year. This allows sufficient time for the many
events to transpire during the siege as described in Jeremiah 32,
33, 34, 37, and 38.

While Ezekiel was faithfully and graphically portraying to
the exiles in Babylon the inevitability of Jerusalem's fall, Nebuchadnezzar's forces drew near to the city. The very day the
siege began, Ezekiel's wife died (Ezek. 24:1, 15-24) — a drastic
sign to the exiles that Jehovah's sanctuary, "the desire of your
eyes," was doomed. In the meantime, Jeremiah was suffering
intensely at the hands of his countrymen in Judah, who considered him to be a traitor for counselling surrender to Babylon.[14]
As a reward for his faithfulness in delivering God's Word without compromise, Jeremiah was plotted against by the citizens
of his own home town (Jer. 11:18-23), beaten and put into the
stocks (Jer. 20:1-3), publicly challenged by false prophets (Jer.
28:1-11), thrown into various prisons (Jer. 37:15, 21), and even
lowered into a deep cistern full of mire (Jer. 38:6).

Several months after the siege began, Pharaoh Hophra came
up into Judah with a large army; and the Babylonians, perhaps
recalling the serious losses they suffered at the hands of Pharaoh
Necho in a clash at the border of Egypt in 601 B.C.,[15] decided
to withdraw from Jerusalem temporarily. In the meantime,

---

[14]Compare Jer. 18:18; 20:7-10; 21:1-14; 25:8-11; 27:1–28:17; 29:24-
32; 32:1-5, 28-36; 34:1-5, 17-22; 37:7-10, 17-19; 38:1-6, 17-23.

[15]Cf. Donald J. Wiseman, *Chronicles of Chaldean Kings*, p. 29.

24. Painting of Nebuchadnezzar's Babylon showing the bridge over the Euphrates, the great ziggurat and the temple of Marduk. Courtesy, Oriental Institute.

25. Painting of Nebuchadnezzar's Babylon showing the Procession
Way passing through the Ishtar Gate. Courtesy, Oriental Institute.

Zedekiah and the people of Judah had agreed under pressure to release their Hebrew bondservants in obedience to God's law (cf. Exod. 21:2-11); but when the Babylonian army withdrew, they immediately broke their covenant (Jer. 34:8-21)! Therefore, God assured them that the Egyptians would depart permanently and the Babylonians would destroy the city even if their army consisted of nothing but wounded men (Jer. 37:6-10; 34: 22; Ezek. 17:17).

The final months of the siege of Jerusalem brought Zedekiah to the edge of despair. Secretly and frequently calling for Jeremiah to hear some encouraging word from Jehovah, he was given the clear alternative: surrender to Nebuchadnezzar and not only live in peace but save Jerusalem as well; or keep on resisting and be totally shattered by the Babylonians (Jer. 37:16-17; 38: 14-23). The Chronicler tells us that one of the reasons why God judged Zedekiah is that "he humbled not himself before Jeremiah the prophet speaking from the mouth of Jehovah" (II Chron. 36:12). The story of this confrontation between God's weeping prophet and the fickle and godless king of Judah is almost without comparison in Scripture for its tragic overtones. Vacillating between the demands of his nobles on the one hand, and a superstitious fear of Jehovah on the other hand, Zedekiah permitted Jeremiah to be alternately humiliated and protected (Jer. 32:1-5; 37:21; 38:10). The pitifully irresponsible puppet ruler of Judah was therefore directly responsible for the destruction of Jerusalem and the Temple (Jer. 38:23).

The end came swiftly and the picture is sickening to contemplate. On July 18, 586 B.C., the city walls were breached and the enemy moved in.[16] Zedekiah and some of his leaders fled

---

[16]Donald J. Wiseman writes: "The severe nature of the final siege of Jerusalem in 589-587 B.C. is shown by the utter devastation of Judah which took place at this time. In the debris of the guardroom by the city gate of Lachish eighteen inscribed potsherds were found. Some, invoking the name of Yahweh, mention restriction of movement and the 'princes who weaken the hands,' perhaps the very opponents of Jeremiah. The majority were messages passing between Hosha'yahu, the commander of an outpost, and Ya'ush, military governor of Lachish. Letter No. IV ends: 'and let my lord know that we are waiting for the fire-signals of Lachish according to the indications which my lord has given, because we

toward Jericho, but were easily overtaken by the Babylonians who promptly dragged them to the main military headquarters at Riblah in Syria. Standing before the mighty monarch to whom he had sworn loyalty in the Name of Jehovah, Zedekiah was forced to watch his sons and the chief priests and the nobility of Judah being slain before his eyes. Then he was blinded so that the memory of this horrible scene would never depart from him (Jer. 39:6-7; II Kings 25:6-7, 18-21). Jeremiah had warned Zedekiah that he would look into the very eyes of Nebuchadnezzar (Jer. 32:4; 34:3); but Ezekiel prophesied that he would not see Babylon with his eyes (Ezek. 12:6, 12, 13). These

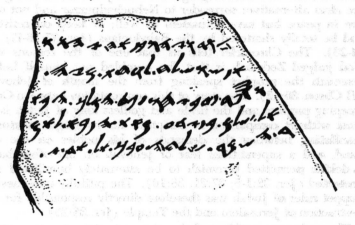

26. Drawing of an inscribed ostracon from Lachish. This letter, written in cursive Hebrew of the time of Jeremiah, was found in a small guard-room under the gate-tower of Lachish, c. 589-87 B.C. Courtesy, Inter-Varsity Fellowship.

cannot see (the fire-signals of) Azekah.' Jeremiah (6:1; 34:7) mentions 'fire-signals' and tells how Lachish and Azekah were focal points in the Babylonian campaign. Lachish, Bethshemesh and Debir, which showed signs of increasing poverty after the war of 597 B.C., now fell, their gates and fortifications were pulled down, the buildings set on fire and the sites, as in many other places in Judah, were abandoned or only sparsely inhabited thereafter. No town in Judah has been found to have been continuously occupied throughout the exilic period." — *Illustrations from Biblical Archaeology*, pp. 70-73.

prophecies were fulfilled to the letter when Zedekiah saw Babylon's king, but entered the city of Babylon both bound and blinded.

In the meantime, the starved survivors in Jerusalem, reduced in some cases to cannibalism by the prolonged siege (Lam. 4: 8-10; cf. Jer. 37:21; 38:9; 52:6), were brutally mistreated by Babylonian soldiers (Lam. 5:11-13; II Chron. 36:17; Jer. 38:22-23), and then herded together and chained like wild animals for deportation to Babylon (Jer. 39:9; 40:1).[17] The only ones that were not deported were poor country people who were left to care for vineyards and orchards (Jer. 39:10); Gedaliah to serve as the governor of this pitiful remnant; certain guerilla fighters who had been hiding in the hills (Jer. 40:7-8); and a few other Jews who had fled to surrounding countries and were now returning (Jer. 40:11-12).

As for Jeremiah, Nebuchadnezzar gave strict instructions that he was to be well cared for (Jer. 39:11-14) because of his great help to the Babylonians in weakening Jewish resistance (cf. Jer. 38:4).[18] Doubtless many deserters had spoken to the Babylonians of Jeremiah's impassioned sermons; and it also seems possible that Daniel warned Nebuchadnezzar against mistreating this great prophet of Jehovah. In the general confusion that followed the fall of the city, however, Jeremiah was accidentally put into chains and led five miles north to Ramah before the error was discovered and he was released (Jer. 40:1-6). Not only was he given the choice to stay or to leave, but he also received a food allowance and "a present" (Jer. 40:5). If his own nation rejected him, God had other means of honoring His faithful servant in a material way.[19]

This public honoring of Jeremiah by the Babylonians must

---

[17]According to Jer. 52:29, over eight hundred Jews were taken captive the year before Jerusalem fell. In addition to these apparently, were many Jews who had deserted to the Babylonians (in response to Jeremiah's appeals?). Zedekiah was particularly afraid of falling into the hands of these deserters (cf. Jer. 38:19; 39:9).

[18]In a similar way, Daniel was honored by Cyrus after the fall of Babylon in 539 B.C. (Dan. 6:2-3).

[19]Cf. Matt. 13:57 — "A prophet is not without honor, save in his own country, and in his own house."

have been the final proof to many Jews that Jeremiah was indeed a traitor (cf. Jer. 37:11-15). But the tears he shed over the fallen city (Lam. 1:16; 2:11, 18); his refusal to leave the land when given the opportunity to enjoy great honors in Babylon (Jer. 40:4); and his lengthy and vigorous denunciations of pagan Babylon (Jer. 50-51), must have made it perfectly clear to all unprejudiced minds that Jeremiah, so far from being a traitor, was the embodiment of God's deep love for His people.

From August 15 to 18, about a month after the city was taken and the captives deported, a Babylonian general named Nebuzaradan began the systematic destruction of Jerusalem (II Kings 25:8; Jer. 52:12). The walls were broken down; the Temple, palace, and chief houses burned to the ground; and all the sacred vessels that had not been taken in 605 B.C. and 597 B.C. were now processed for shipment to Babylon. Even as Ezekiel described the reluctant and gradual departure of the Shekinah Glory from the Temple seven years earlier (Ezek. 8–11), so now the inspired writer takes a final sad look at his beloved Temple, lingering over the details of its destruction (Jer. 52:17-23).

But the measure of tragedy was not yet full. Two months after the city was burned, Gedaliah, the worthy governor of Judah,[20] and many people with him, were brutally slain by an ambitious Jewish prince named Ishmael (Jer. 41:1-10). Johanan, a guerilla captain, had warned Gedaliah about Ishmael, but to no avail (Jer. 40:13-16). Now Johanan's forces succeeded in rescuing Jeremiah and others from the hands of Ishmael; and fearing reprisals from the Babylonians, led the entire group of survivors down to Egypt against the strong protests and warnings of Jeremiah (Jer. 41:11–43:7). "It is difficult to conceive any situation more painful than that of a great man, condemned to watch the lingering agony of an exhausted country, to tend it during the alternate fits of stupefaction and raving which precede its dissolution, and to see the symptoms of vitality disap-

---

[20]Presumably Gedaliah was a friend of Jeremiah, because his father Ahikam once rescued Jeremiah from certain death (Jer. 26:24; cf. 39:14; 40:5-6). It was for this reason that Gedaliah did not oppose Babylonian rule and thus was placed in a position of authority. It was because he trusted unworthy men that he lost his life.

pear one by one, till nothing is left but coldness, darkness, and corruption."[21]

The first phase of Israel's experience as a divinely-established theocratic kingdom on earth had come to an end. The period of Babylonian captivity and of Gentile dominion now began; and Jehovah's purposes for His people Israel took a new course. "For the children of Israel shall abide many days without king, and without prince, and without sacrifice . . . afterward shall the children of Israel return, and seek their God, and David their king, and shall come with fear unto Jehovah and to his goodness in the latter days" (Hos. 3:4-5).[22]

Why did God permit Judah to suffer the horrors of Babylonian captivity? The Chronicler lists three reasons. *First*, Zedekiah refused God's Word through Jeremiah and broke his oath to Nebuchadnezzar (II Chron. 36:12-13). *Second*, the priests and the people adopted heathen customs, polluted the Temple, and scoffed at God's prophets (II Chron. 36:14-16). And *third*, God's provision for the sabbatical year (cf. Lev. 25:4; 26:34) had been neglected for centuries; therefore, "as long as it lay desolate it kept sabbath, to fulfill threescore and ten years" (II Chron. 36:21).

The history of Israel from Solomon to the Babylonian Exile is a four-hundred year demonstration of God's faithfulness to His Word in both promise and warning. He is a God who never changes (Mal. 3:6). He can be depended upon from generation to generation. And what He proved Himself to be for Israel, He proves Himself to be for us, as we heed His warnings and put our complete trust in His gracious promises. "Now these things happened unto them by way of example; and they were written for our admonition, upon whom the ends of the ages are come. Wherefore let him that thinketh he standeth take heed lest he fall . . . but God is faithful . . ." (I Cor. 10:11-13).

---

[21]Quoted from Streane's commentary on Jeremiah by G. Campbell Morgan, *Studies in the Prophecy of Jeremiah* (London: Oliphants Ltd., n.d.), p. 9.

[22]For a thorough study of the future phase of Israel's experience as a theocratic kingdom, see Alva J. McClain, *The Greatness of the Kingdom* (Chicago: Moody Press, 1968), pp. 135-515.

BIBLIOGRAPHY

Aharoni, Yohanan and Avi-Yonah, Michael. *The Macmillan Bible Atlas*. New York: The Macmillan Company, 1968.

Archer, Gleason L., Jr. *A Survey of Old Testament Introduction*. Chicago: Moody Press, 1964.

Baly, Denis. *The Geography of the Bible*. New York: Harper and Row, 1957.

Baxter, J. Sidlow. "Judges to Esther," *Explore the Book*, II. Grand Rapids: Zondervan Publishing House, 1960.

Bright, John. *A History of Israel*. Philadelphia: Westminster Press, 1959.

Bruce, Frederick Fyvie. *Israel and the Nations*. Grand Rapids: Wm. B. Eerdmans Publishing Co., 1963.

Davis, John J. *The Birth of a Kingdom*. Winona Lake, Indiana: Brethren Missionary Herald, 1970.

Douglas, J. D. (ed.). *The New Bible Dictionary*. Grand Rapids: Wm. B. Eerdmans Publishing Co., 1962.

Edersheim, Alfred. *The Bible History: Old Testament*. 2 vols. Grand Rapids: Wm. B. Eerdmans Publishing Co., 1949.

Finegan, Jack. *Handbook of Biblical Chronology*. Princeton: Princeton University Press, 1964.

----------. *Light from the Ancient Past*. Princeton: Princeton University Press, 1959.

Free, Joseph P. *Archaeology and Bible History*. Wheaton, Ill.: Van Kampen Press, 1950.

Guthrie, Donald; Motyer, J. Alec; Stibbs, Alan M.; and Wiseman, Donald J. *The New Bible Commentary: Revised*. Grand Rapids: Wm. B. Eerdmans Publishing Co., 1970.

Harrison, Roland Kenneth. *Introduction to the Old Testament*. Grand Rapids: Wm. B. Eerdmans Publishing Co., 1969.

Jamieson, R.; Fausset, A. R.; and Brown, D. (eds.). *Commentary on the Whole Bible*. Grand Rapids: Wm. B. Eerdmans Publishing Co., 1948.

Josephus, Flavius. *Complete Works*. Trans. by William Whiston. Grand Rapids: Kregel Publications, 1960.

159

Keil, C. F. and Delitzsch, F. *Biblical Commentary on the Old Testament: The Books of the Kings.* Grand Rapids: Wm. B. Eerdmans Publishing Co., 1950.

———. *Biblical Commentary on the Old Testament: The Books of the Chronicles.* Grand Rapids: Wm. B. Eerdmans Publishing Co., 1950.

Kitchen, K. A. *Ancient Orient and the Old Testament.* Chicago: Inter-Varsity Press, 1966.

Krummacher, F. W. *Elijah the Tishbite.* Grand Rapids: Zondervan Publishing House, n.d.

Laetsch, Theodore. *Bible Commentary: Jeremiah.* St. Louis: Concordia Publishing House, 1952.

La Sor, William Sanford. *Great Personalities of the Old Testament.* Westwood, N. J.: Fleming H. Revell Co., 1959.

McClain, Alva J. *The Greatness of the Kingdom.* Chicago: Moody Press, 1959.

Maclaren, Alexander. *Maclaren's Expositions of Holy Scripture,* vol. 2. Grand Rapids: Wm. B. Eerdmans Publishing Co., 1952.

Merrill, Eugene H. *An Historical Survey of the Old Testament.* Nutley, N. J.: The Craig Press, 1966.

Nichol, Francis D. (ed.). *The Seventh-day Adventist Bible Commentary,* vol. 2. Washington, D.C.: Review and Herald Publishing Association, 1954.

Payne, J. Barton. *The Theology of the Older Testament.* Grand Rapids: Zondervan Publishing House, 1962.

Pfeiffer, Charles F. *The Divided Kingdom.* Grand Rapids: Baker Book House, 1967.

Pfeiffer, Charles F. and Harrison, Everett F. (eds.). *The Wycliffe Bible Commentary.* Chicago: Moody Press, 1962.

Pritchard, James B. (ed.). *Ancient Near Eastern Texts.* Princeton: Princeton University Press, 1955.

Thiele, Edwin J. *The Mysterious Numbers of the Hebrew Kings.* Rev. ed. Grand Rapids: Wm. B. Eerdmans Publishing Co., 1965.

Thomas, D. Winton. *Documents from Old Testament Times.* New York: Harper & Row, 1961.

Unger, Merrill F. *Archaeology and the Old Testament.* Grand Rapids: Zondervan Publishing House, 1954.

————. *Israel and the Aramaeans of Damascus*. London: James Clarke & Co., Ltd., 1957.

Whitcomb, John C., Jr. *Chart of the Old Testament Kings and Prophets*. 4th rev. ed. Chicago: Moody Press, 1968.

Whyte, Alexander. *Bible Characters*. Vol. III: *Ahithophel to Nehemiah*. London: Oliphants, Ltd., n.d.

Wiseman, Donald J. *Chronicles of Chaldaean Kings*. London: The Trustees of the British Museum, 1956.

————. *Illustrations from Biblical Archaeology*. Grand Rapids: Wm. B. Eerdmans Publishing Co., 1958.

Wood, Leon James. *Elijah, Prophet of God*. Des Plaines, Ill.: Regular Baptist Press, 1968.

Young, Edward J. *My Servants the Prophets*. Grand Rapids: Wm. B. Eerdmans Publishing Co., 1955.

————. *Studies in Isaiah*. Grand Rapids: Wm. B. Eerdmans Publishing Co., 1954.

NAME INDEX

163

SCRIPTURE INDEX